THE TACTICAL OPTION INVESTOR

USING OPTIONS AS A TACTICAL ALLOCATION TOOL TO ENHANCE PORTFOLIO RETURN

KENNETH ROBERTS

CreateSpace Independent Publishing Platform
North Charleston, SC

CONTENTS

ABOUT THE AUTHOR

I have been in the securities business for over twenty years now. Over the course of my career, I have earned NASD series 3, 6, 7, 9, 10, 56, and 63 designations. That means that I have worked as a stockbroker, commodities broker, and proprietary trader and been a branch manager for a major Wall Street firm. I have been seriously involved in options for over fifteen years and was one of the top option producers in my firm.

I completed advanced options training at my old brokerage firm, the New York Institute of Finance, and paid $14,000 to go through Larry McMillan's personal tutoring program. I have read countless books on option trading, followed several newsletters, and studied many different software programs. More importantly I have been trading options daily for over fifteen years.

The path to profitability was not easy. I've been through the hard knocks that most options traders experience, and I have learned from them. I've read the false hype and claims of spectacular returns from the so-called option gurus that plague the Internet. I've learned a lot of my lessons the hard way. In 2000 I took a small speculative trading account up 143 percent in just over three months and then proceeded to lose all of it when the dot-com bubble burst.

What I have learned and learned very well is that options can be used to manage stock portfolios and produce good returns while lowering risk. I have been successful with options for many years now and generated consistent profitable returns. I can help people learn how to use options and therefore not go through the tough school-of-hard-knocks learning process that I did.

INTRODUCTION

This book is written for serious investors who want to understand how to use options to enhance the return from their portfolios, not for the speculator who thinks he can make a fortune starting with a small trading account. You won't find any get-rich-quick schemes in here or promises of spectacular returns. What you will find are some ideas that will help you get rich slowly, produce income from your investments, and find some ways to hedge a stock or an exchange-traded fund portfolio against a serious market decline. Though written for the advanced or intermediate investor, this book will also provide an introduction to basic investment concepts for neophytes.

Options can be used to generate profits in bull, bear, or sideways markets. In the world of options literature, investors can be bombarded by books and newsletters that claim they can consistently deliver exceptional returns. One of the most common pitches is that 90 percent of their trades are profitable. This may be true, and once you've learned about delta, you'll find that it's easy to sell out-of-the-money calls and puts and have a 90 percent win rate. But what the literature is not telling you is that the 10 percent that lose take away all of the profits and then some. In option investing we consider not just the probability of a trade winning, but also the risk-reward ratio and expected return. Later in the book, we'll discuss how to construct a diversified portfolio using options to enhance return and how to use options to manage risk in concentrated equity positions and existing portfolios.

Chapter One:

WALL STREET: A HISTORY OF FRAUD AND GREED

Why take charge of your own account and learn how to control risk? Even though investing in common stocks is one of the best ways to get a good return on your dollar, in order to be successful, you have to be aware of the history of fraud and corruption on Wall Street. Only through education can you protect yourself from fraud.

Ever since the New York Stock Exchange was formed in 1792 by a group of twenty-four stockbrokers with the Buttonwood Agreement, Wall Street has been full of scandals that disadvantage the small investor. Throughout the history of Wall Street, there has been one scam after another, sometimes by large, supposedly reputable investment firms, sometimes by small boiler-room operations running so-called pump-and-dump schemes. The early stock manipulators bought shares, drove up the price, and then dumped them to an unsuspecting public once the price had been driven up. Then they stood back and watched the price collapse and small investors get wiped out. Today pump-and-dump schemes still persist in the microcap, or penny stock, arena and net fraudsters billions of dollars. Fraudsters will buy up shares in a penny stock that is worthless, and then hire boiler-room salespeople to call and encourage unsuspecting investors to buy due to some outlandish prospects for the future of the company. As new investors buy in, the scammers sell off their shares for a profit. Once the scammers have sold out their stock, the price collapses. Don't think that these old-fashioned pump-and-dump schemes are a thing of the past: you'll see hundreds of offers on the Internet today for these penny-stock newsletters. Here's a recent quote:

> *"Washington, D.C., Feb. 18, 2011* — The Securities and Exchange Commission today charged a group of seven individuals who perpetrated a fraudulent pump-and-dump scheme in the stock of a sham company that purported to provide products and services to fight global warming."

In 1938 thousands of spectators lined up at Grand Central Station in New York to see Richard Whitney, president of the New York Stock Exchange, sent off to Sing Sing prison for embezzlement—the former president of the NYSE, and it turns out he's a criminal.Fraudulent schemes occurred on a regular basis on the next few decades. During the eighties and nineties, Prudential was investigated by the Securities and Exchange Commission (SEC) for defrauding investors in their limited partnership offerings. The dollar amount of the fraud was close to eight billion, at that time the largest in US history. Approximately four hundred thousand investors had losses from the improperly sold limited partnerships. Prudential settled with investors for $330 million and paid another $41 million in fines. This type of punishment is merely a slap on the hand and considered a cost of doing business by many of the largest firms that everyday people entrust their money to.

The majority of the time, if a big Wall Street bank is accused of violating a law, it simply pays the fine, without admitting or denying guilt. In 2003 every major US investment bank, including Merrill Lynch, Goldman Sachs, Morgan Stanley, Citigroup, Credit Suisse First Boston, Lehman Brothers Holdings,

JPMorgan Chase, UBS Warburg, and US Bancorp Piper Jaffray, was found to have defrauded investors through faulty research and conflicts of interest between the company's investment-banking clients and its research departments. The firms were fined a staggering total of $1.4 billion by the SEC.

The mutual fund late-trading scandal of 2003 prosecuted by New York state attorney general Elliot Spitzer included several major fund companies, notably Janus, Alliance Capital, Banc One, Canary Capital Partners LLC, Invesco, Bank of America's Nation's Funds, Prudential Securities, Putnam Investments, and the Strong Funds. The way a late-trading scandal works is that hedge funds are allowed to enter orders after the market is closed for the day. In the United States, mutual fund prices are set once daily at 4:00 p.m. eastern standard time. Late trading occurs when traders are allowed to purchase fund shares after 4:00 p.m. at that day's closing price. Under law, most mutual fund trades received after 4:00 p.m. must be executed at the following day's closing price, but because some orders placed before 4:00 p.m. cannot be executed until after 4:00 p.m., brokers can collude with investors and submit late trades as if they had been placed before 4:00 p.m. Such trades can be made with information about after-hours market developments in other countries, giving the late trader an unfair advantage over everyday long-term investors.

Late trading was illegal under SEC regulations prior to 2003, and Spitzer determined that the Martin Act can be interpreted to prohibit late trading as well. The profits earned by the late traders hurt the annual returns of the fund's investors. Canary Capital Partners settled the complaint for $40 million, while neither admitting nor denying guilt in the matter. Sound familiar? Bank of America stated that it would compensate its mutual fund shareholders directly for losses incurred by way of the illegal transactions. This is typical of the way many large firms operate: they rip off their investors, pay a fine and pay some compensation to the investors they hurt if they get caught, and then move on to the next profitable scam at the expense of the small investor. Sometimes people's life savings get wiped out, yet the big corporations go on, with their fat profits and huge bonuses.

In March 2009 Bernie Madoff pleaded guilty to eleven federal felonies. He defrauded investors out of billions of dollars through the most massive Ponzi scheme in history. At one time Madoff was the president of the NASDAQ and was highly respected in the industry. Madoff founded the firm Bernard L. Madoff Investment Securities LLC in 1960 and was its chairman until his arrest in 2008. The firm was one of the top market makers on Wall Street. The frightening thing about the Madoff Ponzi scheme was the scope—almost $50 billion—and the fact that Madoff had been another highly regarded Wall Street leader who turned out to be nothing more than a sophisticated robber. J. P. Morgan, though he has denied complicity, may have also benefitted from the scheme by collecting almost $1 billion in fees and charges over the life of the fund.

In March 2011 Rajat Gupta, a former member of the board of Goldman Sachs and a board member of Proctor & Gamble, was charged with insider trading in what may become one of the largest insider-trading cases ever. The SEC has charged that Gupta passed information to Raj Rajaratnam of the Galleon Group about Goldman's earnings and about a $5 billion investment Berkshire Hathaway Inc. made in Goldman. Galleon reportedly made about $900,000 from the transaction. Gupta has not been charged with a crime yet, but he may be subject to nothing more than the old slap-on-the-wrist fines.

The common investor has been ripped off time after time to the benefit of the big banks and brokerage houses, and today's markets are more complex than ever. Information travels around the world in seconds. Supercomputers calculating millions of pieces of data place high-speed orders and execute rapid-fire trades for small profits across global exchanges. It has been said that approximately 50 percent of the trades on the exchanges today are from some form of algorithmic or programmed trading. In the past a do-it-yourself investor could look at market depth and get a pretty good idea where the large block trades were placed. Today dark pools and algorithmic trading dominate, and tape reading is not what it used to be.

Investors should also use caution using hedge funds. The 1998 blowup of Long-Term Capital Management is a case in point. Run by some of the best and brightest traders in the world (two of its managers were Nobel Prize winners), the firm still ran into difficulties and had huge losses. One dollar invested in Long-Term Capital in March 1994 had turned into over four dollars by April 1998. But by October 1998, those four dollars had turned into less than forty-five cents. The dollar losses were over $3.5 billion. The problem with being invested in a hedge fund when it runs into trouble is that the losses can be total because of the leverage used. Also, instead of depending upon the stability of a broad-based index for returns, the hedge fund investor is relying heavily on the skills and expertise of the fund managers, and if they make an error, the results can be catastrophic. One alarming thing about the Long-Term Capital Management debacle is that here we have an example of some of the brightest minds and best traders in the business making mistakes and experiencing near-total losses. Their leverage was so great that their failure put the entire financial system in jeopardy, and they had to be bailed out by a consortium of large banks. The average investor cannot afford near-total losses and hope to recover, so risk must be controlled constantly.

The Granite Partners hedge fund managed by David Askin declared bankruptcy in April 2004. Askin had invested in CMOs using three-to-one leverage, and the losses came to $1.6 billion. In those days mortgage-backed securities were roughly one-third of the total bond market and were considered to be relatively safe. In 1994 we had a small, unexpected rise in interest rates, and Askin's CMO funds collapsed. The 1994 crash would turn out to be a salient warning for the 2008 crash, but apparently the lesson wasn't learned. Probably because there was just too much money involved, too many profits to be made.

Pershing Square IV, run by well-known fund manager William A. Ackman, who ran Pershing Square Capital Management, suffered huge losses on a fund Ackman started solely to bet on the rise of the stock price of discount retailer Target. The fund lost almost 90 percent of its value.

Hedge funds in general contain some inherent risks. One is that since their disclosure requirements are minimal, investors don't have the transparency they need to analyze their strategy on an ongoing basis. When hedge funds started, most of them actually hedged and traded pairs of stock, short one and long the other; with their leverage, they made some decent returns and had some good risk control. As time went on, more and more investors discovered that if they were right, they could make a lot more money without the hedge and took on trades with more and more risk in an effort to get great returns. Today if you place money into a hedge fund, you are hoping that the manager's skills will pay off. Don't be fooled by fancy resumes or stellar track records: even the best managers can take on too much risk and blow up all of your hard-earned capital.

Don't think that by investing only in the equities of large, substantial companies you are avoiding risk. Individual equities can also contain substantial risks even if they seem to be solid companies based on fundamental analysis. WorldCom at one time was the second largest long-distance phone carrier in the United States, behind only AT&T. WorldCom overleveraged and declared bankruptcy, and the stockholders were wiped. Another one of many examples of leading companies that collapsed is Enron. Enron was one of the world's leading energy, commodities, and services companies, based in Houston. Before its collapse in 2001, Enron employed over twenty thousand and claimed revenues of nearly $101 billion. *Fortune* magazine named Enron "America's Most Innovative Company" for six consecutive years. But at the end of 2001, it was discovered that its reported financial status was sustained substantially by accounting fraud. Enron has since become a symbol of willful corporate fraud and corruption. The scandal also brought into question the accounting practices and activities of many corporations throughout the United States and was a factor in the creation of the Sarbanes-Oxley Act of 2002.

With this in mind, tactical option investors always maintain a healthy skepticism of fundamental research reports; they will also study the price action of a stock and keep a careful eye on basic indicators like the put-call ratio and insider-selling activity. We never take on a position in an individual equity where our portfolio cannot sustain a total loss in that equity.

How can investors shield themselves from this type of fraud and abuse? The best thing investors can do is educate themselves and manage their own portfolios or work with a registered investment adviser (RIA) whom they trust and establish a good working relationship with that adviser. It's always better to work with a registered investment adviser than a broker because the investment adviser has a fiduciary responsibility to handle each account with the utmost care. In addition you, the client, pay the adviser directly. The adviser receives no additional compensation from mutual fund companies, insurance companies, or corporations issuing debt or equity. Brokers, on the other hand, are compensated by the investment companies, not by the client, and the result of that can be high expenses, hidden charges, and a variety of bewildering commission structures. It is best to use low-cost index funds or individual equities and avoid paying high fees for a managed fund that also has the potential for some form of fraudulent activity. It's easy to conclude from the history that the SEC is not capable of stopping all forms of fraudulent activity before they happen.

Tactical option investors try to minimize risk and maximize return at all times and in every way possible. One way to minimize risk is to use broad-based index funds for equity exposure and avoid low-priced speculative stocks and managed funds with high expense ratios. Investing in low-cost, broad-based index funds or sector-based funds can eliminate company-specific risk entirely. The tactical option investor uses exchange-traded funds, also known as ETFs, to avoid late-trading scandals and to be able to take advantage of opportunities in the marketplace during the trading day when they exist. When we invest in individual equities, we practice position sizing: any position taken on will be a maximum percentage of the portfolio and will not exceed that. For investors fortunate enough to have large, concentrated equity positions from employer stock or inheritance, we'll discuss ways to protect those positions and avoid the potential for disaster.

Considering Wall Street's history of criminal activity, one might ask, why even bother? Why invest in stocks when corruption is rampant in the system? Well, the answer is simple. Common stocks provide the best long-term return of any investment vehicle. Wall Street has also been a center of financial innovation and development. Today's fully electronic markets and variety of investment choices give investors speed and flexibility that just a few years ago traders would not have dreamed of. Options are one of the few areas where the small investor has an advantage: while it can be extremely difficult for a large institution to effect transactions in sufficient quantity for its portfolios, the small investor can be very nimble and get optimum pricing on most trades.

Chapter Two:

UNDERSTANDING INVESTMENT BASICS

This is a chapter that sophisticated investors may want to skim or skip altogether. Why invest in stocks in the first place if they can be risky? Remember when gas was fifty cents? Common stocks have historically provided the best return and can help your dollars maintain their purchasing power due to inflation. If there was no inflation, you could stuff your money under your mattress and not be concerned about future purchasing power. Because of inflation, investing in stocks is the best way to keep your investment dollars growing.

Besides stocks, you can invest in bonds. High-quality bonds, like those issued by the US Treasury, pay some interest and will have their full value at maturity. Though bonds are safe, they don't provide much room for growth to keep up with the effects of inflation.

Diversification means that you don't put all your eggs in one basket. You invest in both stocks and bonds and some commodities.

While the stock market is the best source of long-term returns, it can be risky over shorter time frames. We can see short periods of time with negative returns and times when the market loses substantial value in very short time frames, like a couple of days or even hours.

Typically the younger a person is the more he should invest in stocks, even though there can be periods of negative return.

As a person ages and gets closer to retirement and has accumulated a fairly large portfolio, he can no longer withstand large market declines and should move more of his funds to bonds for safety and to produce some income.

Target-date retirement funds will change the ratio of stocks and bonds as the investor ages, being more aggressive when retirement is a long ways away and becoming more conservative as the investor approaches retirement and enters his retirement years.

One way is to also invest in other assets besides stocks and bonds; these assets can include gold, silver, oil, natural gas, cotton, sugar, and other resources. You can also invest in currencies of other countries, so if the value of the dollar is declining, you can have some of your funds in currencies that may be appreciating, like the Swiss franc, Japanese yen, or Canadian dollar. The problem with inflation and retirement planning is that you have to be prepared to pay more for things you'll need in the future. One way to cover this is to invest in the things you'll be consuming, like gas, oil, and foods like sugar and meat. If you own unleaded gasoline in a fund and the price increases, the increase can offset the increase you see at the gas pump. If you own a commodity like sugar in your investment portfolio, the price increase can offset what you have to pay for groceries at the store.

This process is known as tactical asset allocation. In times of high stock market risk, tactical investors will reduce the stock part of the portfolio. The method we use to determine where to invest and how to balance a portfolio is known as relative strength. What we do is monitor all markets to see which prices are the strongest. We invest in the markets with the strongest rising prices and rotate to stay in the strongest markets. We strive to lower risk in every way we can, including investing in low-cost, diversified exchange-traded funds and making portfolio adjustments by considering the investor's age and market conditions.

The most common investments are stocks and bonds. If you own a stock, you own a part of the company that issued it and have a claim on the future cash flow of that company. If it pays a dividend, you are entitled to receive those funds. If it goes up in value, you participate. The investor also bears all of the risk of stock ownership if it declines in value. With a bond, the investor is loaning money to the issuer and expects to receive a coupon payment and her money back when the bond matures. Bonds are issued by corporations, the federal government, and state and local governments. Investors may also choose to place funds into commodities. Commodities can be separated into several distinct categories, including precious metals, energy, and agricultural resources. Foreign currencies can also be an attractive place to invest and can provide further diversification compared to having all of your assets valued in US dollars.

There are different ways to make investments in any of the categories mentioned above. You can own individual stocks and bonds. You can also purchase futures contracts on precious metals or buy gold and silver coins. Futures contracts can be bought on oil, natural gas, or unleaded gasoline. Foreign currencies contracts can be bought on a futures exchange, or you can buy the actual paper currency and store it safely somewhere.

Investors can make the individual investments or use mutual funds. Mutual funds provide diversification and, in the case of actively managed funds, also have professional management. Mutual funds can be open-end or closed-end. An open-end fund will create more shares when you make a purchase. Open-end funds can have a sales charge in the form of a commission or can be no-load, meaning they are commission-free. In either case they will still have an expense ratio that should be considered before one invests in a fund. Equity index funds will mirror an index like the S&P 500 and will have no commission plus very low expense ratios—typically under 0.20 percent or 20 basis points. Actively managed funds can have sales charges as high as 5 percent up front and still have annual expense ratios over 1 percent. A closed-end fund has a set number of shares, then trades daily on an exchange at either a premium or discount to its net asset value, or NAV. A sales commission is paid to the brokerage when a closed-end fund is purchased, and these funds will also have annual expense ratios.

The exchange-traded fund, or ETF, is a fund type that we'll talk about much more in later chapters and what we'll use for portfolio construction and option strategies. The ETF universe is expanding rapidly and allows an individual investor to purchase stocks, bonds, gold, oil, or foreign currencies. Almost any investment vehicle is available today by purchasing an exchange-traded fund.

Chapter Three:

TYPES OF RISK AN INVESTOR FACES

Counterparty Risk

Counterparty risk is the risk that the counterparty of your fund will not perform. Hedge funds, for example, have high counterparty risk. Numerous funds with high-profile managers with great track records have gone belly-up. Hedge funds can be particularly disastrous when they fail because of the leverage they employ. Many funds have had total or near-total losses due to miscalculations on the part of their managers. Probably the most famous example is that of Long-Term Capital Management, a firm that was run by Nobel Prize winners and whose losses were over $3 billion and nearly 100 percent. We reduce counterparty risk by using low-cost, broad-based index ETFs. ETFs still contain risk, but the counterparty risk is minimal, especially when compared to that of a hedge fund.

Systematic Risk

Systematic risk is defined as a risk to an entire financial system. If the entire system goes through a shock or collapse, even broad-based index funds will suffer, and the meltdown can go through multiple asset classes simultaneously. Diversification can help, and hedging can definitely help control systematic risk. Owning long put contracts can be one of the best ways to hedge against systematic risk.

Nonsystematic Risk or Company-Specific Risk

Nonsystematic risk, also known as company-specific risk, is the risk of one company failing due to multiple reasons, including product failure, lawsuits, fraud, and the like. Wall Street's history is full of stories of once substantial companies failing completely. WorldCom was the second largest long-distance carrier in the United States, behind only AT&T; Enron was one of the world's leading energy companies. Both stocks imploded and became worthless. This kind of risk can be diversified away. We control company-specific risk by using broad-based index ETFs. If one company within the S&P 500 fails, there may very well be some fallout, but the overall index of 500 stocks will still go on.

Contagion Risk

Contagion risk is similar to systematic risk but is defined as a scenario in which one financial event leads to another, which eventually leads to a meltdown. The US subprime crisis of 2008 at first appeared to be limited to the US housing market, but it eventually spread to lending liquidity and bank reserve requirements and went overseas to Europe and Asia. Stocks plunged and investors fled to safe investments like US Treasuries. Contagion can be diversified away to some extent by holding treasuries in your portfolio and by hedging.

Inflation Risk

Inflation risk is one of the worst types of risk an investor can face. Though not as shocking to a portfolio as a market crash, the steady erosion of your purchasing power over time can have devastating long-term effects. The way to combat inflation risk is to invest in securities whose return exceeds the rate of inflation, which means investing in equities. Adding commodities to a portfolio can be a good inflation-risk hedge because many commodities can keep pace with inflation. An inflationary period combined with a market crash can be especially devastating to a portfolio. The value of an equity portfolio can decline dramatically at a time when an investor needs extra funds to keep up with inflation. We aim to control inflation risk by moving into the strongest sectors of the market and rotating out of them as conditions change.

Interest-Rate Risk

Bond investors have to be concerned about interest-rate risk. In general, as interest rates rise, bonds fall and vice versa. Individual bonds have a set price that they will mature at, but between the time they are issued and the time they mature, their market values will fluctuate with interest rates, kind of like a playground seesaw. Longer-term bonds will fluctuate in price more than shorter-term bonds. The duration of a bond is a formula based on the coupon rate, price, and maturity, and longer-duration bonds are more volatile than shorter-duration bonds. Bond funds can decline in value as interest rates rise because the fund itself has no set maturity even though the bonds within the fund do. In a rising-rate environment, one way to control risk is to shift to shorter durations.

Credit Risk

Bond investors must also be aware of credit risk, which is based on the credit worthiness of the issuing institution. Bonds are rated by rating agencies, which can give a pretty good idea what the risk is, but the rating agencies can make mistakes. Mortgage-backed debt was considered to be relatively safe, and many mortgage-backed obligations had high credit ratings prior to the housing bubble burst of 2007.

Pin Risk

Pin risk is a term that is understood by professional options traders but generally not very well understood by the investing public. Covered call writing is the most basic of all option strategies and is widely used by many investors. It has been proven that covered call writing can reduce risk and enhance return in a portfolio. In today's low-interest-rate environment, more and more investors are turning to covered call writing as a way to produce some needed income from a retirement account.

When a covered call is written, there are two scenarios that can unfold at option expiration. If the underlying stock or ETF is above the call option strike price, the stock will get called away. If the price of the underlying stock is below the strike price of the call option, the call option will expire worthless.

So what happens if you are very close to option expiration and the underlying stock is right at the strike price? The answer is that you can't be sure whether or not the stock will get called away. This is not an issue if you don't care whether the stock gets called or not. But it can be a major problem if you want to get called and don't. For example, say you bought one hundred shares of ABC at $45.00 and sold the $50.00 call for $1.00. The stock is over $50.00 on the last trading day prior to expiration. In this situation, you want the shares called away from you. You either need the capital for another investment or no longer want the stock in your portfolio due to deteriorating fundamentals or technical analysis. With thirty minutes to go on the Friday before expiration, the stock is at $50.05. It looks like it should get called, but what happens if the stock settles right at $50.00 or moves below in the final seconds of trading? You may end up holding a stock that you wanted to get rid of. You could think that the stock is going to get called only to find out on Monday morning that you still own it and that it has gapped down at the open, creating a substantial loss.

The best way to eliminate pin risk is to close out positions on the last trading day before option expiration to be sure that you have the result you want. You can buy back the calls for a few cents and sell the stock in the open market if you want it called away. The same applies to any other short position, like puts, spreads, and so on. You should close the position if the underlying is very close to the option strike price near expiration if the unexpected option assignment or lack of an assignment will create problems for you.

Chapter Four:

OPTIONS EXPLAINED

What is an option? An option is a contract written on an underlying investment vehicle. There are options on stocks, futures, indexes, and exchange-traded funds. We are going to focus on stock and ETF options. There are two types of option contracts, calls and puts. There are also two parties to each contract: the buyer of the option, known as the holder, and the seller of the option, known as the writer. The holder of a call option has the right but not the obligation to purchase the underlying. The writer of a call has the obligation to sell the underlying. The holder of a put has the right to sell the underlying and the writer of a put has the obligation to purchase the underlying.

In market jargon if you buy an option, you are considered to be *long* that option contract. If, on the other hand, you sell an option, you are considered to be *short* that option contract. If you sell and are short the option, you can be either covered or uncovered. The market term for uncovered option positions is *naked*. So if you sell a call on a stock where you already own the underlying, you are considered to be covered, and that is known as a covered call. If you sell a call and do not own the underlying, then you are short a naked call; the risk of such a position is potentially unlimited. Remember, if you buy a call, you have the right to buy the underlying stock at the strike price of your call contract. If you sell a call, you are required to deliver the underlying stock at the strike price of the call contract. If you sell a naked call and the stock price rises dramatically due to a merger announcement or new product announcement, the losses can be severe. If you have seen options literature that suggests you can have 90 percent winners, that is the kind of risk they are taking on. There are always option contracts available that have a 90 percent probability of being out of the money at expiration. It's the 10 percent that end up in the money that create substantial losses.

Tactical option investors who use options to manage and enhance returns on stock and ETF portfolios control risk at all times. We do not ever use positions that have unlimited risk, even if the probability of success is very high. When we employ option positions, it is to enhance the performance of our portfolio, so we use only those option positions that have a defined risk. Though there are only two types of option contracts, calls and puts, they can be put together in numerous ways to create complex positions based on one's outlook for the market. There are spreads, straddles, strangles, butterflies, condors, and more. Later in the book, we'll discuss these various strategies, how they relate to market conditions, and how they can be strategically employed along with an existing portfolio.

All option contracts have a set expiration date and a predetermined price that the transaction will be executed at, known as the strike price. Most liquid options have a wide selection of strike prices to choose from. The liquid issues, like most ETFs, now trade in one-dollar price increments. Stocks over one hundred dollars in price trade in five-dollar increments. If the strike price is the same as the current stock price, that option is referred to as being *at the money*. If a call option has a lower strike price than the current price, that option is *in the money*. If a call option has a higher strike than the current price, that option is considered to be *out of the money*. A put option is the opposite: if the strike is lower than the current price, it is out of the money, and if the strike is higher than the current price, it is in the money. The position of the option strike relative to the current underlying price is known as the moneyness of the option. If you purchase an out-of-the-money option, you want the price of the underlying to move so that the option will be in the money. If you sell an out-of-the-money option, you want the price of the underlying to stay where it is or move away so your option stays out of the money and eventually expires worthless or can be purchased for a profit.

There are four different types of transactions used to trade options. You can sell to close, buy to close, sell to open, and buy to open. There are three different scenarios if you own a long option: you can sell your option prior to expiration, you can exercise your option, or your option can expire worthless. Most options have an automatic exercise feature, which means that if a long option is in the money at expiration, it will be automatically exercised for you by the clearing firm. If you are short an option, likewise there are three possibilities: you can buy the option back for a profit or a loss, you can let the option expire, or you can get assigned the contract. Option contracts have two different styles of exercise, American and European. With an American-style option, the holder of the contract can exercise her right to buy or sell at any time. European-style options can only be exercised at expiration. If you have sold an American-style call on an issue that pays a dividend and that option is in the money, you have a very good chance of getting an early assignment and having to deliver the shares prior to the ex-date of the dividend.

Currently, options are issued long term, known as long-term equity anticipation securities (LEAPS), up to three years out. They are also issued quarterly, monthly, and—a recent development—weekly. The option contract will expire on a predetermined date. In addition to the standardized option contracts, there are FLEX options. FLEX options can be customized to the strike price, expiration date, and exercise style. The expiration date on a FLEX option can go all the way out to fifteen years. Strike prices can be at any price in penny increments or may be specified as an index level or a percentage or by using other methods to define a numerical deviation from an index level. FLEX options can be especially useful for investors who are fortunate enough to own large, concentrated equity positions because of the customization available.

The option that an investor may select depends on market opinion, goals for the investment, and the price and liquidity of the option. An investor with a bullish opinion on a stock or ETF may wish to buy a call option. When a call is purchased, the investor has risk limited to the price of the call and unlimited upside potential to infinity. Stocks really can't go up all the way to infinity, but they can have large upside gains, so the real potential can be substantial. A bullish investor may also wish to sell a put. If a put is sold, the potential reward is limited to the price of the put, also known as the premium, and the risk is unlimited all the way to the stock going down to zero. One way to think of owning a call option is that the investor will participate in the upside of stock ownership with less risk and greater leverage than owning the stock outright. The risk is limited to the premium paid for the option, and the premium also provides the leverage. If you pay $2 for an $110 call on a $100 stock and the stock rises to $130, your call will be worth $20 at expiration, and you will have increased your investment by ten times with $2 at risk. If you bought one hundred shares at $100, that would require $10,000, and if it went to $130, you'd get a 30 percent return with $10,000 at risk. With the call option, you would get a 900 percent return with $200 at risk.

An investor with a bearish opinion might want to purchase a put. When a put is purchased, the risk is limited to the premium paid for the put. The potential reward is substantial, and the stock can become worthless. A bearish investor may also choose to sell a call. If a call is sold, the potential reward is limited to the premium received for the call, and the risk is potentially unlimited if the stock makes a large move to the upside. When you own a put, you'll participate in the downside of a stock with less risk than you would if you were to short the stock. For example, if you short a $100 stock, you have to have a margin account and be willing to accept the risk of the stock exploding to the upside. If you purchase the put option, the most you can lose is the premium paid for the put, but you have the potential to gain if the stock declines all the way down to zero.

To determine the theoretical price of an option, an option-pricing model is used. Buyers and sellers on the marketplace determine the actual price constantly throughout the trading day. The most commonly used pricing model is the Black-Scholes model. From the Black-Scholes model, we can derive some calculations used to determine how an option price will react to market variables known as the Greeks (because letters from the Greek alphabet are used to designate them). The delta is the rate of change of option price with a corresponding one-point move in the underlying instrument. The underlying instrument will always have a delta of 100. I like to express the delta in terms of the number of shares of the underlying that you hold. If you are long one hundred shares of XYZ, then you have a positive 100 delta position. If you are short one hundred shares of XYZ, then you have a negative 100 delta position.

When you combine complex option and stock positions, you'll have to keep track of the deltas, which are additive. At-the-money options will have a delta of about 50. So if you own one hundred shares of XYZ and decide to sell an at-the-money call with a delta of 50, your net position delta will now be 50 (100 - 50 = 50). This means that as long as the delta of the short call remains at 50, your combined position will behave like fifty shares of the underlying, not one hundred shares, so the risk of ownership in the underlying is reduced by a fifty-share equivalent. As call options move into the money, the delta will increase; as they move out of the money, the delta will decrease.

The delta is also roughly equivalent to the probability of the option being in or out of the money at expiration. An at-the-money option will have a delta of about 50, which means that it will move half of what the underlying moves, but it also has a fifty-fifty chance of being in the money at expiration. A long call will have a positive delta, and a long put will have a negative delta. Conversely the short call will have a negative delta, and the short put will have a positive delta position. The gamma is the rate of change of the delta with a corresponding one-point underlying move.

The vega, or lambda, is the change in option price due to a 1 percent increase or decrease in implied volatility. Vega is the most commonly used symbol; however, it is not a Greek letter, so some practitioners prefer to use lambda. The two can be used interchangeably. Short-term options will have a lower vega and will not be as sensitive to changes in implied volatility. Longer-term options will have higher vegas, and their price will be much more sensitive to changes in implied volatility.

The theta is the rate of decay of an option's price over time. Long option positions, whether they are calls or puts, will have a negative theta, which means that time will work against the holder of an option through the process of price decay. Short options will have a positive theta, which means that the option writer or seller can earn slow profits over time through the price-decay process. Shorter-term options will have a higher theta than long-term options, and their price can decline rapidly through decay in the final weeks or days to expiration. Longer-term options will have a lower theta and a lower rate of price decay. The rate of price decay accelerates rapidly as the option approaches expiration. Covered call writers who sell call options for income usually do better by selling short-term options and benefiting from the rapid price decay. In-the-money options will also have a lower theta and less time value than at-the-money options. Out-of-the-money options that have no intrinsic value will have a relatively high theta. The rho is the change in an option contract's price due to a change in interest rates.

It's not necessary for an investor to understand the derivation of the Black-Scholes model or other option-pricing models, but it is important to understand the Greeks and how to monitor the various types of risk in an option position. Most of the trading platforms these days have the Greek calculations built right into the option-trading platform so investors can consider the impact of the Greeks prior to entering a trade and monitor the Greeks during the lifetime of the trade. The Black-Scholes model assumes a lognormal distribution for stock returns. Actual studies of the return data show more quiet days than the lognormal distribution would account for and also that huge moves occur more frequently than statistics would predict. In the crash of 1987, the market fell about ten standard deviations. The lognormal distribution would say that a ten-standard-deviation move is basically impossible, yet in the marketplace huge moves occur with greater frequency than the option-pricing model can comprehend.

In addition to being familiar with the Greeks, it's important to have some understanding of basic statistics, especially standard deviation and lognormal distributions. I closely monitor the volatility or standard deviation of the equities and ETFs that I trade. There are four different types of volatility to evaluate. Future volatility is your estimate of what the volatility will be going forward, typically the period that is the life on the option contract. If the underlying has been through a period of low volatility, you may expect it to rise; if it's been through a period of very high volatility, you may anticipate the volatility will quiet down for a while and consider limited-risk strategies that will capitalize on lowering volatility. Historical volatility is the standard deviation of the past history of the underlying. The tactical option investor will study the historical volatility to help determine what may happen with the future volatility. The third type of volatility is forecast volatility, which is a forecast of what the future volatility might be. Currently, New York University (NYU) has a free online volatility lab—known as Vlab—that provides volatility forecasts. The current URL is http://vlab.stern.nyu.edu/. Based on the work of Nobel Prize winner Robert Engle, the site uses GARCH models and provides forecasts for most major indexes and heavily traded stocks. These three types of volatility are all related to the underlying instrument, the stock or ETF. The fourth type of volatility, implied volatility, is related to the option contract. It is determined by consensus of all of the participants in the marketplace and is derived from the Black-Scholes options-pricing model.

When looking at a quote of an option price, check the implied volatility of the option compared to the historical volatility of the underlying. Is it significantly higher or lower? If it is, check the newswire to see if there's a reason for the pricing. If the implied volatility is high and you're looking at a stock, check to see when the next earnings release date is or if there's a major product announcement or lawsuit pending. When I am considering entering an option position, I'll check the implied volatility of the options under consideration. I'll pay close attention to the relationship between the implied volatility of the option and the historical volatility of the underlying investment. I'll consider the current standard devi-ation plus some longer-term history of the range and trend of the volatility. In addition to looking at the current implied volatility of the option, I'll also look the longer-term history of the implied volatility of the options. I guess we could call that the historical implied volatility. Since the implied volatil-ity is the current volatility priced into an option, when you trade an option, you are essentially making a forecast of the future implied volatility. If you think that the implied volatility is too low and will rise, you should consider a strategy that will profit from rising volatility—like a long straddle—if you want to be direction neutral or delta neutral. If you believe that the implied volatility is too high and that the volatility will decline in the future, you should use a position that will profit from falling implied volatility, like a credit spread or iron condor or iron butterfly.

Implied volatility is the one element of the Black-Scholes model that must be estimated. Implied volatility can be derived from the formula using the current market price. Options that have a high implied volatility will be expensive, and options that have a low implied volatility will be considered cheap. In general we want to sell something that's expensive and buy something that's relatively cheap. So if you're bullish on a stock, believe that the stock price is reasonable, are willing to own it, and think that the option price is high due to the implied volatility, it may be a good time to sell a put. If you're bearish on a stock, believe that it is overvalued, and think that the options are cheap due to low implied volatility, you may wish to purchase a put. Conversely if you're bullish and think the implied volatility is low, you may want to buy a call. If you're bearish and think that implied volatility is high, you may want to sell a call.

Often-Repeated Misconceptions about Option Trading

Options should only be used by professionals.

The use of options by nonprofessionals has become more widely accepted over the last several years. Today's modern retail brokerage platforms and tight option spreads put individual investors on the same playing field as the pros. Numerous studies have shown that using options can enhance return and lower risk in your portfolio.

Options should only be used in an IRA or tax-deferred account.

Some people think that, due to possible high turnover, using options can create a tax headache. That also is not true. Options can be bought or sold long term, and the portfolio turnover is something that can be controlled. Today's tax reporting software makes it very simple to report investments even if you do have high turnover, like from a strategy of selling covered calls on a monthly basis. The IRS will allow an investor to attach a realized gain/loss statement from a brokerage instead of completing the schedule.

Individual investors get taken advantage of in trade execution.

In the old days, the market makers controlled the game, and the bid-ask spreads were wide. Today's electronic markets are very efficient and competitive. Many issues now trade in penny increments. Investors no longer get taken advantage of by the market makers.

Option trading only works when markets are volatile.

Options can help enhance the return on your portfolio regardless of whether the volatility is high or low. There are different strategies that can be used to profit or protect your portfolio when the volatility is rising or when the volatility is falling.

Option trading is not for young investors.

Some people say that option trading is good only for highly sophisticated investors with years of experience and a high net worth. That is another misconception. Younger investors with a growth objective may want to purchase long-term options on the market or an individual stock to participate in the upside of the market but limit their downside risk to the amount of the premium paid for the option.

The trades are hard to execute and require experience.

Another common falsehood. Today's modern platforms and options chains make it quite simple to enter trades with very little room for trade errors. It only requires a little learning to be able to execute option trades.

Brokerages that are good for options are not suitable for equities or ETFs.

Not true. Today the mainstream brokers all have pretty good option platforms, and the firms that specialize in options also have some very good platforms for stocks and ETFs.

You need to spend a lot of time and money on options-trading education.

That's another one that may have been true at one time but does not apply anymore. Most of the brokerages have some good educational materials. The Options Industry Council (OIC) has some excellent free education on its website. The Chicago Board Options Exchange (CBOE) also has a wealth of free information. There are many books worth studying as well.

Options traders are greedy short-term speculators.

Nothing could be further from the truth. Options can be employed by long-term investors to reduce risk and produce income. Cash-secured puts can be sold to target an entry price on a stock or ETF for a long-term hold, and the returns can be favorable. Covered calls can be used for income generation in today's record low-interest-rate environment.

Options trading popularity will die off.

The volume in options trading has been expanding recently. The ETF explosion has led to more and more options volume. The use of options is becoming more widely accepted than ever and will continue to increase.

Forecasting Volatility

With all of the different types of volatility discussed above, you may find yourself wondering how and why one should have a forecast of future, historical, or implied volatility. Most investors spend their time trying to forecast the direction of the market or of an individual stock. Followers of the buy-and-hold random-walk theory know that the market has a strong upside bias over long time periods and will buy low-cost index funds and hold them indefinitely. Most investors will buy a stock thinking that over time it will appreciate in price and maybe pay some nice dividends along the way. Technical analysts will devote time to studying charts, looking at things like moving averages, stochastics, and other indicators to attempt to forecast a future price or at least the direction of the price in the future. Fundamental analysts will study earnings reports and the trend of the reported earnings and use things like price-earnings multiples and book values to determine the future value of a stock. Most investors devote the vast majority of their analytical efforts to studying company reports or charts of past price action to determine the future price of a stock or index. So why would anyone be interested in forecasting the future volatility of a stock?

The first reason is that the volatility of a stock or index generally has an inverse relationship to its price. This is because prices have a tendency to fall faster than they rise. If the volatility is increasing, the price is usually declining, and if the volatility is falling, the price is generally rising. So if we could forecast volatility accurately, that would also tell us something about the likely future direction of the stock. There is a great deal of statistical evidence that stock prices do follow a random walk. In other words, the current price reflects all of the known information about the company, and there is no correlation between past prices and prices in the future.

The second reason is that volatility is possible to forecast. When analyzing volatility, we find that there is a serial correlation between returns. Volatility has a tendency to manifest itself in clusters. The price of a stock goes up or down and may show signs of trending predominately in one direction or another, but the price movements are random. However, if you study a chart of the volatility of a stock, you'll immediately notice that there are distinct periods of high and low volatility, that the periods of high volatility are followed by periods of lower volatility, and that the periods of low volatility are interrupted by high-volatility periods. There's a simple reason for the clustering of volatility. In the absence of significant news, a stock may quietly drift higher for a long period of time. If some news like a potential lawsuit, a product recall, or a new product announcement by a competitor comes out, the stock may sell off quite rapidly until the news is fully digested by the investing public. These short-term sell-offs can be considered to be buying opportunities for investors wishing to accumulate shares of the stock. When we chart the volatility of the stock, these news events will show brief spikes in the volatility that typically persist for short periods of time and then return to normal. At times like this, the future price direction may not be simple to forecast, but the volatility can be because it is a very good assumption that the volatility will eventually revert to the mean or return to a more normal level. The tactical option investor will utilize periods of high volatility to produce more income or do some share accumulation.

Special Dividends and Call Option Contracts

There are times when option contracts are adjusted for corporate events like stock splits or special dividends. In the case of a two-to-one stock split, for example, the option contract strike price is adjusted in half, and the number of contracts is doubled.

There is no contract adjustment for ordinary dividends. Regular dividends that are paid on a quarterly basis are factored into the option's price. When a stock goes ex-dividend, the stock's price is adjusted by the amount of the dividend. The price of the call and put options reflects the amount of the dividend.

Due to the ongoing fiscal cliff negotiations, many companies are opting to pay out special dividends this year before the anticipated increase in the dividend tax rate. Currently dividends get a special tax rate of 15 percent. That rate could go as high as 39.6 percent in 2013, depending on the outcome of the fiscal cliff negotiations. Campbell Soup Company became the last major company to declare a special dividend. Over one hundred companies with a market cap greater than $240 million have declared special dividends this year. The total value of all the dividends is almost $23 billion.

If you're using a covered call or a collar strategy to collect dividends, remember that with these special dividends, the strike price will be adjusted downward to reflect the special dividend.

Strategy Bias

One of the keys to success in trading options or in using options to enhance return on a portfolio is having some flexibility in your strategy selection so you can adapt to rapidly changing market conditions. I have talked with many traders over the years that have a strategy bias, and they get good results for a while only to eventually experience a period of heavy losses and a substantial drawdown of capital.

Strategy bias means that the trader learns one strategy and uses it on a regular basis regardless of market conditions. A strategy like the iron condor is a good example. People learn about the iron condor and understand that it can have a high probability of success, but they may not have much experience with dynamic delta hedging and thus learn the hard way that iron condors also have a poor risk-reward ratio.

Strategy bias doesn't account for so-called regime changes, cycles in which the market moves from a period of relative quiet through a period of high volatility. Iron condor traders can have losses when the market moves from low volatility to high volatility. In 2008 when the volatility spiked to extreme levels, iron condor positions hit their maximum loss.

If you are forecasting rising volatility, you'd want to consider a trade like a long straddle. Long straddles can be effective when there is a known event approaching that could move the market. On Thursday May 31, the SPY closed at $131.47. The monthly jobs report was released premarket on Friday June 1, and the SPY opened at $129.41 and hit a low of $128.16. A long straddle bought before the close on Thursday—with the knowledge that the jobs report was coming—could have produced some nice profits. In contrast, an iron condor held through that would have had an adverse movement.

To be successful over time, you need to master several different strategies and learn how to employ them in changing market conditions.

Chapter Five:

OPTION TRADING STRATEGIES

The Long Call

The long call is probably one of the simplest option positions to understand. The purchaser of a call is considered to be long the position. The long call gives the investor exposure to the upside of the market while the risk is limited to the premium paid for the option. Long calls will have a positive delta and a negative theta. Long-term equity anticipation securities, or LEAPS, can be purchased up to three years out. If you are bullish on the market, for example, but concerned about global events like sovereign debt defaults, war, or terrorism, you could purchase LEAPS on an index like the S&P 500. If the market rises, you'll participate. If an unexpected event occurs and the market takes a big hit, your risk will be controlled because what you paid for the option is much less than what you would have paid had you purchased the index fund outright.

Considerations to be made when purchasing a long call include the price of the underlying, the implied volatility of the option, and the strike price, expiration, delta, and theta (or decay factor) of the option. Remember, the rate of decay accelerates rapidly in the final weeks prior to expiration. Investors buying call options as a limited-risk stock substitute should use longer-dated contracts to give the underlying more time to make the anticipated move and to minimize the negative effects of time decay. The options delta is also a primary factor to consider. The at-the-money call will have a delta near 50, which means that the option will move half of what the underlying does. Out-of-the-money calls have lower deltas as they move out of the money. They also have lower prices. While this equates to less capital at risk, investors will need a larger price movement in the underlying to profit. The delta is roughly equal to the probability of the option being in the money at expiration, so a call with a low delta, say a 25-delta call, will only have a 25 percent probability of being in the money at expiration. An in-the-money option will have a higher delta but will also have a higher price, meaning more capital at risk. An in-the-money call with a 75 delta will have a 75 percent chance of being in the money at expiration. If the price of the underlying rises, that call's delta will change at a rate given by the gamma and will go to 100 if the option goes deeper into the money. Generally, tactical option investors buy high-delta, in-the-money calls that have a high probability of success as a stock or ETF substitute. When buying deep-in-the-money calls, however, it almost never makes sense to pay more for the call than you would to purchase the underlying on margin, or 50 percent of the price of the underlying.

The Covered Call

The covered call is one of the most common strategies employed by individual investors. The covered call writer is moderately bullish to neutral in his market opinion and is willing to sacrifice some upside gain in order to collect the premium from the sale of the call contract. The risk of the underlying stock position is reduced by the amount of the call premium received. Call premium is received into the investor's account as immediate income. For example, an investor may buy one hundred shares of XYZ stock at $25.00 and subsequently sell one $30.00 call at $1.25. At expiration if XYZ is above $30.00, the investor will have the stock called away. If XYZ is below $30 at expiration, the investor will keep the shares, any gain between $25.00 and $30.00, and the call premium of $1.25.

Her cost basis in the stock is now reduced to $23.75, the initial price of the stock minus the premium received for the call.

Numerous studies have been done on the covered call strategy, and one of the conclusions drawn from them is that covered call writing cannot only enhance portfolio return, but also provide those returns with lower risk. The volatility of the underlying fund or stock can be significantly reduced by employing a covered call writing strategy. Since the delta of an at-the-money option is 50 and the delta of the underlying fund is 100, if an investor sells an at-the-money option, the position delta is reduced to 50. That position has about half the risk of the underlying position as long as the option stays at the money and the price of the underlying does not move very much.

Another Greek that the covered call writer wants to monitor closely is the theta, or rate of decay. The theta tells the option writer how much money she'll earn daily just through price erosion. At-the-money options will have the highest theta. Say, for example, that an investor sells a slightly out-of-the-money option for $2.00 at the beginning of the month (not the first calendar day of the month, but the first Monday following the third Saturday of the month). If the underlying price stays steady or declines slightly in the last week of the option's life, it may be only worth $0.05. Since the option's theta is now only $0.05 and the investor has already earned $1.95 in profit, it may make sense to buy that option back, sell the following month's slightly out-of-the-money option, and try to increase the theta of the holding. In other words, you should attempt to increase the daily income earned through option decay. Below is a risk graph for a covered call position on the SPY, which is the ETF that tracks the S&P 500.

Covered Calls—Managing the Trade

If you're thinking about using covered calls for income, you'll want to consider how you're going to manage your trades from the time you establish them until option expiration.

If you already hold the underlying stock or ETF, it's only a matter of selecting the strike price and expiration of the call option that you wish to sell and entering your order. When you enter the order, you are faced with the decision of what order type to use. Most traders will choose between a market and a limit order when selling calls. Though you may have read elsewhere that you should only use a limit order when trading options, I don't agree with that. I've found that I get excellent executions with market orders as long as the stock is a very liquid penny pilot issue. The most liquid ETFs have excellent execution on market orders, and there are times when a market order is better. For instance, let's say your stock has a rapidly falling price. If your limit isn't going to get hit, you'll have to go through the process of canceling and replacing. And if the underlying has fallen, you'll have to settle for a lower price than you would have with a market order. If the stock or ETF that you're selling the call option on is not very liquid and has wide bid-ask spreads, don't use a market order; instead, use a limit and place it about halfway between the bid and the ask, and then give it time to get filled. The thinner the trading is, the more patient you have to be with the order getting filled.

If you don't already own the position in the underlying, you have some more choices. One choice is to sell a cash-secured put and then wait until you get assigned to begin the call-writing process. Another choice is to use a buy-write ticket. With a buy-write ticket, you enter a simultaneous order to buy the stock and sell the call option at a net debit. So if the stock is trading at $25 and the option is selling for $1, you'd enter an order for a net debit of $24. You can also use market orders with buy-write tickets, and they'll work as long as the underlying is very liquid. If the underlying is not very liquid and has wide spreads, you should use a limit order for sure. If you don't want to use a buy-write, then first you purchase the underlying security, then sell the call option. If you like to trade a little bit to try to enhance returns, you can leg into the position by buying the stock, letting it run up, and then selling the call if the stock begins to drop.

Once you have a covered call position established, two things can happen at expiration. The price of the underlying will be above or below the strike price, and either you will get called or the option will expire worthless. If your option is in the money prior to expiration and you decide you want to keep the stock, you'll have to buy the calls back, then sell more at another expiration date. If you roll the calls for a credit—that is, you sell them to open for more than you but to close—you can keep rolling them until they expire worthless and generate a profit. You'll also need to watch out for your dividend ex-dates. If your option is in the money prior to the ex-date and the expiration date is close by, there is a very high probability that you'll get called. If you want to hold the stock and collect the dividend, you'll need to roll for a credit prior to the dividend ex-date instead of waiting for the expiration date. If you decide you want to sell the stock prior to the call option expiring, you'll probably want to buy the option back and then sell the stock. Depending on your level of option approval at your brokerage, you may have to buy the call back first. If your approval level is high enough for naked calls, you'll need to consider whether you want to assume the risk of an uncovered call position.

Before you establish your first position, have a plan in place for how you are going to manage the trade, and know your dividend ex-dates.

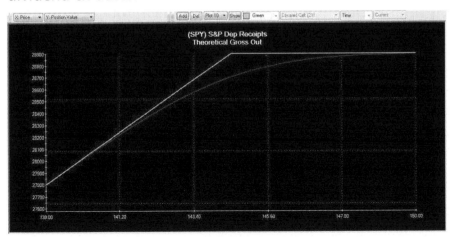

Advanced Call-Writing Strategies
Delta-Neutral Call Writing
Much has been written about the popular covered call writing strategy in which an investor will purchase one hundred shares of a stock or an ETF and sell one call option for some income and partial downside protection. The term *covered call* means that for every option you sell, that option contract is covered by one hundred shares of the underlying investment.

Advanced option traders will be familiar with the term *delta neutral*. For those readers who are not familiar, the term means that your position has no market directional bias; in other words, the position is neutral to market movement. If we buy one hundred shares of XYZ stock, that position alone will have a delta of 100. If we sell an at-the-money call with a delta of 50, because we are short the call, it will have a negative delta, so the net position delta will be 50 (100 deltas for the one hundred shares of XYZ stock and -50 deltas for the short XYZ call). This is how your typical covered call position works. If you were to sell an out-of-the-money call with a delta of 25, your net position delta would be 75; in other words, the total position would behave like 75 shares of the underlying instead of 100.

Now, if we want to create a market-neutral position, we'll sell enough calls so that the net position is delta neutral. So if we buy one hundred shares of XYZ again, we could sell two 50-delta at-the-money calls, three 33-delta out-of-the-money calls, or four 25-delta out-of-the-money calls, and so on. If the net position delta is at or near 0, your position will not have directional risk as long as it remains delta neutral. Then you can earn the theta, or the decay, from the short options. You don't have to sell the options at just one strike price, either. For example, you could sell one at-the-money 50-delta call and two out-of-the-money 25-delta calls.

Once a position is established, the delta will change by the rate of the gamma, and adjustments will have to be made to remain delta neutral. You can adjust the shares of stock you own, sell more calls, or buy some calls back to adjust.

As with any strategy, there are risks: the underlying can drop rapidly before you can adjust, and you can experience a loss. Since you have uncovered short calls, if the underlying explodes upward rapidly, you can also experience a substantial loss. Stocks that have high volatility or may be potential takeover targets should be avoided. Megacap stocks or broad-based index ETFs can be good candidates for a delta-neutral strategy. Indexes can rise and fall rapidly, but they cannot drop all the way to zero the way individual equities can or explode upward the way the stocks getting taken over can.

Looking at some current prices as of this writing, the SPY is at $131.82, and the Feb 135 calls are twenty-one days from expiration. The Feb 135 calls sell for $0.61 and have a delta of 24. You could sell four of those calls against a one-hundred-share position of SPY and take in $2.44 in premium; the theta is -0.03, so you'd be getting $12.00 per day in decay. You could regularly make delta-neutral adjustments as time went on, but you wouldn't have to worry about loss unless the SPY rose to above 135 by expiration. This is not a recommendation for the above SPY trade; I just like using real numbers to illustrate.

The Long Put

The long put is similar to the long call in that the investor has the right but not the obligation to exercise. The purchaser of a put has the right to sell the underlying at the strike price on or before the expiration date in the case of an American-style option or on the expiration date if the investor owns a European-style option. The owner of a put will participate in the downside of the market with risk limited to the premium or price paid for the put contract. Puts can be purchased to profit from a price decline in a stock, an index, or a commodity. For example, if you own an all-stock portfolio with twenty holdings and are concerned about a general price decline in the market, you could purchase a put on a broad-based index that would increase in value if the market declines.

The tactical option investor who purchases a put that is not used to hedge a portfolio against a market decline is considering a couple of different factors. The first is an analysis of the underlying to determine whether it is overpriced. There are a variety of fundamental research sources that can be used to help determine whether a stock or an index may be overvalued. Once we have determined some overvalued investments to consider, then we study the charts and consider the momentum of the investment. An individual stock or a commodity, for example, may seem to be overvalued, but its price momentum can continue upward for long periods, and it can become even more overvalued. By applying some technical analysis, investors can find investments that are overvalued and have some downward price momentum. A moving-average crossover can be a good, simple tool to apply here. The third step is to identify underpriced put options. You can find an overvalued stock in a downtrend, and if you pay too much for the option, it may not produce a profit. To locate undervalued options, you need to consider the historical volatility of the stock and the implied volatility of the option and study the history of the implied volatility to see where the implied volatility is relative to its long-term averages.

The difference between a speculator and a tactical option investor in these types of transactions is that the tactical option investor will have a fundamental opinion on the underlying investment, apply some technical analysis to see whether the price momentum is favorable, and find a reasonably priced option. The tactical option investor will also buy an option with sufficient time remaining in the contract for the price movement to develop. Many option speculators experience failure because they don't take the time to properly analyze these three steps, and they trade in too short a time frame. There is much work to be done when taking directional trades with options; the markets are very efficient, and arbitrage opportunities rarely exist. Using a long put to hedge a portfolio is different because the investor chooses the option contract based on his underlying portfolio and is concerned about portfolio protection or insurance. Puts used for portfolio insurance are known as protective puts. Below is a graph of the risk profile with a long put position. The risk is limited to the price paid for the put, and the gain is unlimited until the stock hits zero.

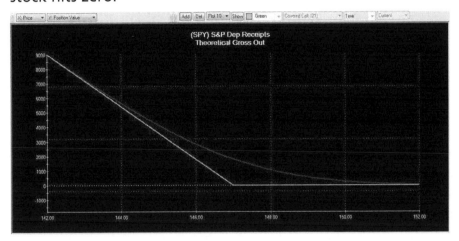

The Protective Put

The protective put is used when an investor is concerned about a decline in his share price but wants to keep the potential for gains. The protective put is like insurance purchased on a stock holding to lock in gains or prevent further loss by purchasing puts. This will increase the total cost basis in the stock by the amount of the put premium. For example, if XYZ is at $50 and you have a cost basis of $25, you could buy a $50 put for $2 for six months. If XYZ goes all the way to zero, like Enron, you have locked in a profit of $23 per share.

Protective puts can also be purchased on indexes to hedge a portfolio. For example, say you have a $250,000 portfolio consisting of twenty stocks. It's a simple matter to calculate the beta of your portfolio relative to a major index like the S&P 500. Then you can determine how many S&P or SPY puts to buy to give your portfolio a hedge against a broad market decline, but not a company-specific decline. If you are a bond investor with a portfolio of US Treasury bonds and want to hold your bonds but are worried about a rise in interest rates, you can purchase put contracts on the IEI, the IEF, or the TLT that will profit if rates rise and the value of the bonds in your portfolio falls. If you're not sure how to select the best options or how to design the hedge to your specifications, consult with a registered investment adviser (RIA) who specializes in options. Most RIAs are not option specialists and have limited experience with option transactions.

The Short Naked Put

The uncovered, or naked, put is sold when an investor wants to produce income and is willing to accumulate shares of stock. The key difference between an investor and a specu-lator when it comes to naked put selling is that the investor is targeting a stock or ETF for a long-term buy and has set a price that he is willing to purchase that stock at. The speculator is trying to profit by selling the put and hopes either it will expire worthless or he can buy it back later for a profit. The investor, on the other hand, is satisfied with either outcome—having the put expire worthless or getting assigned and purchasing the underlying shares at a predetermined price. Income is pro-duced by selling out-of-the-money put options at a price lower than the current price of a stock when the investor would be willing to buy the stock at that price. For example, if XYZ stock is trading at $25, the investor is willing to purchase XYZ at $20. Therefore, she sells a $20 put for $1. If the stock stays above $20, the investor retains premium. If the stock goes below $20, it will be put to the investor at $20. However, the investor already has collected $1 in premium, so her cost basis is $19.

Many sources consider naked put selling a risky strategy. However, selling an uncovered put is not as risky as outright stock ownership. If an investor owns a stock that goes to zero, like General Motors, the investor has a total loss. If the same investor sold a put and was assigned on that put to purchase those GM shares, the investor would have retained the put premium even though the shares eventually went to zero. Naked put selling is riskier to the brokerage houses: they fear that the investor may not meet the margin call if shares are put to her. If the investor utilizes proper position sizing relative to her portfolio and is using the strategy for stock accumulation, uncovered put selling is not a high-risk strategy and in fact has the same risk profile as the covered call strategy, which is generally considered to be low risk. When stock prices decline, implied volatility has a tendency to rise, making the options more expensive. If you're targeting an entry price for a stock and see it decline rapidly, check the option quotes for a rise in the implied volatility and high prices for out-of-the-money puts. When bad news comes out on a stock that you want to own, that can be a good time for selling out-of-the-money puts.

Say you're willing to accumulate one thousand shares of XYZ over time. You could sell ten out-of-the-money puts and wait for the shares to get put to you, or you could use a fraction of the total, say two puts per month, and repeat the process until you've accumulated the full one thousand shares. When selling naked puts, tactical option investors target investments to accumulate with a price below the current market that we're willing to buy them at and try to find puts that are relatively expensive. Puts will have a tendency to be priced high every quarter prior to the earnings release to account for a substantial move in the stock. This increase in the implied volatility can create an opportunity for the put seller. Out-of-the-money puts can have a higher price at this time and provide an attractive entry point.

For investors wishing to accumulate shares in a commodity-based ETF such as USO, the oil ETF, the volatility can be higher before the weekly release of the petroleum report. Stock-index ETFs can have higher implied volatility prior to major releases of economic data like the monthly employment numbers or scheduled Federal Reserve meetings. When selling a put, you can use the delta to approximate the probability of getting assigned at expiration. An at-the-money put will have a 50 delta, so if you sell an at-the-money put, you have a fifty-fifty chance of ending up owning the shares. At-the-money puts also have a relatively high premium and will have high theta. As the puts move out of the money, the delta is lower, so the probability of getting assigned also decreases as you move out of the money. If you sell 20-delta puts, the premium may not be that high, but you'll only get assigned 20 percent of the time, and your entry price into the underlying will be substantially below the current market price. If you are targeting individual equities with this strategy, you will only get assigned when the stock drops significantly, and you may decide you don't want to own that stock anymore. It's critical to be sure you're willing to purchase a stock when selling puts. When this strategy is used to accumulate ETF shares in a broad-based index like the S&P 500, for example, by selling far out-of-the-money puts on the index, you'll only buy shares on dips, and this can be a good cost-averaging strategy for share accumulation in an index fund.

The Married Put

The covered call is probably the most popular option strategy used today. It is very simple. Most investors tend to be long stocks, and the idea of writing a call option, collecting some premium, and being willing to accept a higher price for an underlying equity position appeals to many investors. Covered calls can provide some decent income and limited downside protection while you are waiting for your stock to appreciate to your desired exit price.

The married put is another simple option. Most investors don't short stocks, so the married put is not very commonly used, but it can be a good strategy. The married put is just about the opposite of the covered call. The investor will identify a stock or ETF that he thinks has topped out. The stock is sold short, and then a put option is sold on that position at a price point at which the investor will be happy to buy the stock back. The profits to the downside are limited to the strike price selected and the premium received for the sale of the put. The risk of adverse price movement in the underlying that exists with the covered call exists here, but now it is to the upside. With a married put, the risk is unlimited, and the upside reward is theoretically limited, again similar to that of a covered call.

So if you think that ABC stock won't go any higher, you could short ABC, say at $25. Then you could sell a $20 put, say for $1. If ABC goes below $20, you'll get assigned, buy the stock back at $20, and close out your position for a $6 profit. The percent return that you'll receive depends on the margin rate that you get from your broker.

Shorting stocks isn't for everybody, but the married put can be a viable strategy. As always it's wise to do some thorough research and avoid stocks that could be potential takeover candidates or that could experience rapid price appreciation for some other reason, like a new product announcement or a lawsuit settlement. Investors who rely on technical analysis alone should review the fundamentals to see whether any issues that could impact the price are pending.

The Covered Combination

The covered combination is a return strategy used when an investor is willing to either sell or buy the underlying stock and wants to produce income. The investor who is willing to accumulate stock or sell his holdings can sell out-of-the-money puts and out-of-the-money calls on the existing position. If the stock stays in the range between the strikes, the investor keeps the entire premium. When above the call strike, the stock will get called away, and when below the put strike, the stock will get put to the investor. In either case the investor retains the premium from selling the puts and the calls. So if the stock gets put to you, you pay the strike price for the stock minus the put premium and minus the call premium. If the stock gets called away, you sell the stock at the strike price and retain the call premium plus the put premium. For example, if the investor owns one hundred shares of XYZ at a cost of $25.00, she sells one $20.00 put for $1.00 and sells one $30.00 call for $1.00, making the net premium $2.00. If the stock is between $20.00 and $30.00 at expiration, the investor keeps the entire premium of $2.00. If it is above $30.00, the stock gets called away, and the investor has a gain of $7.00. If it goes below $20.00, the investor will now own two hundred shares of XYZ and have a cost basis of $21.50 on the two-hundred-share position.

The Calendar Spread
The calendar spread is an option strategy that involves simultaneously buying an option and selling an option with the same strike price but a different expiration date. A calendar spread can be long or short. A long calendar spread is done for a net debit, and the risk is limited to the amount of the debit. A short calendar spread is done for a net credit. Investors can use calendar spreads to enter hedged stock or ETF positions. The long put calendar spread can be utilized to enter a long stock position with limited risk. If the investor has a market opinion that the underlying will stay below a certain strike in one month and then rise the following month, a long put calendar spread may be a good choice. Here's how it works. XYZ stock is at 25, and we think it will stay at 25 this month, then rise next month with its earnings report. We're going to sell the near-term 26 put and buy a longer-term 26 put. The net debit is $1. We'll get assigned on the near-term put, then hold a long stock position with an entry price of $27, but we have the right to sell it for $26, so our maximum loss is $1, and our maximum gain is unlimited. If XYZ rises to $30 after the earnings report, we have a gain of $3 and have only risked $1. When there is a volatility skew between the expiration months, we can enter these positions with very tight spreads and very low risk. A volatility skew occurs when different expiration months have higher or lower levels of implied

volatility. In-the-money options will have tighter spreads than at-the-money options but will have a lower probability of success.

Similarly the long call calendar spread can be used to enter a short underlying position with limited risk when one's forecast calls for the underlying stock or fund to decline in value in the future. The spreads can be sold for a profit if they widen or employed as a strategy to enter controlled risk positions for certain time periods. Calendar spreads can also be set up as diagonal spreads. A typical diagonal spread will be long a far-dated in- or at-the-money option and will sell a near-dated out-of-the-money option. A diagonal spread can be used as a covered call substitute with less risk and less capital outlay than owning the underlying security. A long-dated in-the-money call can be purchased with a very long expiration, like a LEAP, and short-dated current-month or weekly out-of-the-money options can be sold against the position for income.

Dual Calendar Spread

The dual calendar spread consists of a put calendar spread and a call calendar spread. It can be put on for a net credit or a net debit. A debit dual calendar spread can be an effective strategy around earnings time. We'll call it an earnings dual calendar, and here's how it works. We want to be long the options that are in the reporting month because we are forecasting a rise in implied volatility in the option price until the report comes out, and then the implied volatility will fall rapidly. We'll be short the contracts that will expire before the earnings release because we know that their implied volatility will drop with their expiration date.

Here's an actual example from the time of this writing. This is not a trade recommendation. Sun Trust Bank, STI, will report earnings on Monday October 22, 2012. We anticipate that the implied volatility of the November options will remain elevated until the earnings announcement. We forecast that the implied volatility of the October options that expire on

October 20, before the earnings announcement, will collapse by the expiration date. We can put this trade on in the first week of October and plan to hold it until the expiration on October 20. Here are some of the key data points:

Size	Exp	Strike	Put/Call	Price	IV	Theta	Delta
+1	Nov 17	28	Put	0.93	31.27%	-1.34	-39.72
+1	Nov 17	29	Call	1.00	29.45%	-1.32	47.22
-1	Oct 20	28	Put	-0.39	27.75%	+1.85	34.31
-1	Oct 20	29	Call	-0.46	25.52%	+1.85	-41.91
			Net Debit	$1.08		1.01	-0.10

So the net debit is $108.00, which is also the maximum risk. For a ten-contract position, that would be $1080.00. The theta is $1.01, which means that for each contract you'll earn the decay of $1.01 per day. For a ten-contract position, that amounts to just over $10.00 per day in option decay. The net delta is -0.10, which is essentially delta neutral. The plan is to close the position on the day of the first expiration before the earnings come out for a net debit greater than $1.08. If the underlying makes a substantial price movement, the position will take on some delta, and a gamma-scalping strategy can be applied to make the position delta neutral again.

Bear Call Spreads
The bear call spread is a vertical credit spread. With a vertical credit spread, the investor will sell a lower-priced strike call option and purchase a farther out-of-the-money call option as insurance to limit risk. The credit received is the premium

received for the short call minus the premium paid for the long call. The maximum risk is defined as the distance between the strikes selected minus the net premium received. The bear call spread is used when your forecast for the underlying is neutral to bearish. To obtain the maximum credit, we want the underlying to stay below the short call so that both options expire worthless and we collect the credit.

Let's look at an actual example that currently has decent profit potential. On April 27, 2012, Amazon (AMZN) closed at $226.85. If we look at the weekly call options that expire on May 4, the $230.00 call will sell for $2.80, and the $235.00 call can be bought for $1.44. The net credit we'll receive is $1.36, or $136.00 per contract. If we set our maximum allowable loss at $5,000.00, we'd use thirteen contracts. The actual maximum loss would be $4,732.00, the theoretical profit or expected return would be $1,453.00, and the maximum profit would be $1,768.00. If AMZN rises to the lower strike at $230.00, we could close out the position or do some dynamic delta adjusting to control loss. The position could be adjusted by adding some long calls or short puts, buying some AMZN stock, or a combination of those. The chart below shows the profit/loss points for this call spread.

Investors who have long-term stock holdings may also want to use a bear call spread to produce income and have potential for upside gain. One of the disadvantages of the popular covered call strategy is that in exchange for the income received from the covered calls, the investor is forced to forgo upside gain. If the underlying fund makes a large upside move, the investor does not participate. With a bear call spread, income is produced by selling out-of-the-money calls and purchasing farther out-of-the-money calls in the same quantity. This way, in the event that the stock makes a large upside move, the investor will participate and still receive some income. For example, if our investor owns one hundred shares of ABC at $25, she could sell one $30 call and buy one $35 call for a net credit. Above $30 the shares would get called away, but she would still own the $35 call. Therefore, if the stock were to rise above $35, she would still have unlimited profit potential from the remaining long call at the 35 strike. Below is a profit/loss graph for the bear call spread. The profit is limited to the initial credit received, and the loss is limited to the spread minus the credit, or the difference between the short strike and the long strike minus the initial credit.

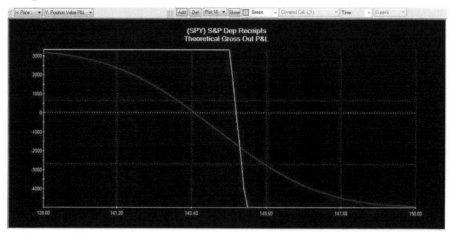

The Bull Call Spread

The bull call spread is a debit vertical spread. The maximum gain is the distance between the strikes minus the initial debit. With a debit spread, the maximum loss is the initial debit. The bull call spread can be used when the investor is moderately bullish and wants limited risk. If XYZ stock was trading at $25.00 and you thought that it was going to reach $30.00 by the next expiration, you could buy one $25.00 call for $1.00 and then sell one $30.00 call for $0.25. Your initial debit to establish the position is $0.75, which is also your maximum risk. Your maximum potential gain is the distance between the strikes: $5.00 minus the debit $0.75, or $4.25. If you were trading ten contracts, you'd be risking $750.00 to try to make $4,250.00. Below is a graph of the bull call spread showing the limited risk and the limited return.

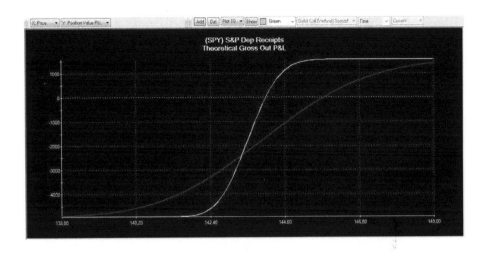

The Stock Repair Strategy

Have you ever bought a stock and seen it go down? One way to try to recover is to use the stock repair strategy. It can be used to lower your break-even point. What you do is sell a call ratio spread on the underlying stock to adjust your cost basis. For example, our investor bought two hundred shares of XYZ at $30.00, and it's now at $20.00. She would sell four $25.00 calls for $0.50 each and buy two $22.50 calls for $1.00. At no cost, the break-even point is now lowered to $25.00.

The Bull Put Spread

Put spreads are vertical credit spreads that can be used when an investor is willing to accumulate stock. Such spreads offer downside protection in case the underlying stock breaks below a predetermined level or when an investor wants to try to earn the credit but have worst-case risk control. The strategy is called the bull put spread. What you do is sell out-of-the-money puts but purchase farther out-of-the-money puts for downside protection in case the stock breaks down. For example, if XYZ is trading at $25, the investor sells one $20 put and buys one $15 put for a net credit of $1. If the stock stays above $20, the investor will keep the credit. If it goes below $20, the stock will be put to the investor, but the investor has downside protection at $15, so the maximum potential loss is capped at $4. The profit/loss graph for a bull put spread is shown below. The profit is capped by the initial credit received to put the position on, and the maximum loss is capped by the width of the spread minus the initial credit.

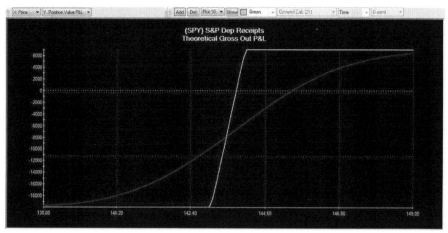

Bear Put Spread

The bear put spread is a vertical debit spread used when the investor is moderately bearish on the underlying. The gain is limited to the distance between the strikes minus the initial debit to establish the position. The loss is limited to the initial debit. If ABC stock was trading at $30.00 and you thought that it was headed to $25.00 by the next expiration, you could buy the $30.00 put for $1.00 and sell the $35.00 put for $0.25. The net debit would be $0.75, and that would be your maximum loss. The maximum potential gain would be the difference between the strikes minus the initial debit: $5.00 - $0.75, or $4.25. The graph below illustrates the profit/loss potential of a bear put spread.

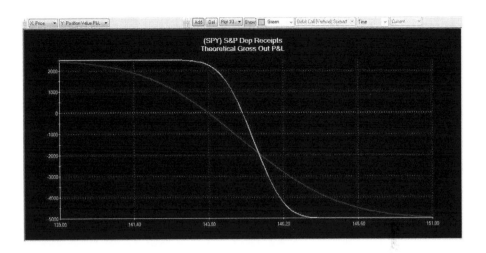

Index Call Spreads

Index call spreads can be used to enhance returns on a stock portfolio. The first step is to look at the portfolio and determine which index it correlates most closely to. A mostly technology stock portfolio may correlate most closely to the NASDAQ, or the QQQ, ETF. A portfolio of foreign stock might have the closest correlation the EAFE or the EFA ETF. For our example, we'll assume that the investor has a $260,000.00 portfolio that is highly correlated to the S&P 500. The ETF for the S&P 500 is the SPY. The next step is to determine how many option contracts represent the value of the portfolio. As of the writing of this book, the SPY is trading at about $130.00, so twenty contracts—(20 × 100) × $130—would equal $260,000.00. The next step is to sell a credit spread on the SPY. If we sell the 133 ×134 spread, we receive a credit of $0.25 or $500.00. The maximum risk on the spread is the amount of the spread minus the credit, which comes to $0.75 or $1,500.00. If the SPY stays below 133, we keep all of the credit. If the S&P declines, the portfolio will decline, and we'll still keep the credit for additional income or an offset to the decline. If the SPY rises above 134 at expiration, we'll have our maximum loss on the spread, but it will be offset by the gain in the portfolio. Say the SPY is at 135 at option expiration. We'll have a loss of

$1,500.00 in the call spread, but if the portfolio is 95 percent correlated to the S&P 500, we'll have a gain of 3.85 percent on the SPY. Assuming the portfolio has a 95 percent correlation to the S&P 500, that translates to a gain of over $9,500.00 in the portfolio.

Using this strategy consistently, the investor will have profits on the spread when the market is flat, declines, or rises slightly. When the market makes a large gain, the investor will have a loss on the spread that is offset by the gain in the portfolio. Strike prices for the spread can be selected using out-of-the-money options that have a low probability of loss. Remember, when a loss does occur, it is offset. Over time there should be more winning months than losing months based on lognormal distribution of market returns, and the strategy will have a positive expected return.

The Iron Condor

The iron condor is a defined-risk market-neutral strategy. It is composed of a bull put spread and a bear call spread put on for a net credit. The risk is defined as the distance between one of the spreads. The investor hopes that the underlying market will stay between the two short strikes and the net credit will be collected as profit. This can be a good income strategy. It can have a high probability of success, depending on the width of the condor or how far the short strikes are from the underlying. It can also have a poor risk-reward ratio, depending on the distance between the short and long strikes on the call and put spreads.

Let's look at an actual example as of the time of this writing. The SPY closed at $137.57. If you had the market opinion that the SPY would not rise by more than $4.43 or fall by more than $5.57 by expiration, you could consider selling an iron condor that would consist of one short 132 put, one short 142 call, one long 145 call, and one long 129 put. The net credit, determined by using the current bid-ask prices and going out forty-one days in time, would be $88.00 for each condor. The risk would be defined as the distance between a spread and the net credit, or $212.00. Volatility is low now, so the option prices are not real high. You can get more credit by widening the distance between the spreads, but then there is also more risk. For example, if you decided to use a four-point spread, it would be for a net credit of $104.00, but now the risk would be $296.00.

Using the standard deviation is a good way to determine where to place the spread; it can be calculated so that there is a low probability that the underlying will move far enough against you, but you'll also have the long positions there for absolute risk control.

The iron condor can be applied when you think that volatility is high and you believe it will fall. If the implied volatility is high in the current month and lower in the farther-out months, a calendar spread might make more sense. A profit/loss graph for a short iron condor appears below.

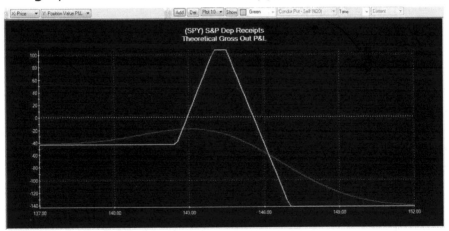

Iron Butterfly

The iron butterfly can also be a good income strategy. It consists of an at-the-money short straddle wrapped up by a long strangle. It has a defined risk, which is the distance between one of the short and long strikes. The maximum return is the credit received at the time the position was initiated. To collect the maximum credit, the investor using the iron butterfly hopes that the underlying will stay right at the strike and not move at all. Below is a profit/loss graph for a short iron butterfly.

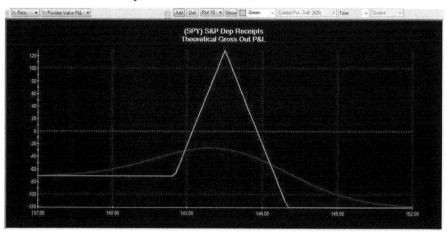

Synthetic Long Stock

Options can be used to create positions that act like the underlying investment. Every underlying, option, and complex option position has a synthetic equivalent. In other words, the tactical option investor can put together option positions that will act similarly to another option or underlying position.

We'll start with a simple one: the synthetic long stock position. A synthetic long stock position will act like a long position in an underlying investment, whether it's an individual stock or an ETF. A synthetic long stock consists of a short put combined with a long call. Remember, we used the long call position when we wanted to participate in the upside of the market and have limited exposure to the downside. We used the short naked put position to accumulate shares of stock. The naked put has profit potential limited to the premium received for the put: if the market makes a large move to the upside, the investor does not participate. The long call will participate in a large upside move but will decay over time if the market is flat and, of course, will decline in value if the market goes down.

The synthetic long stock is generally put on for a credit when the investor is willing to take on the full risk of stock owner- ship. It can also be put on for a debit. The short put is sold, and the long call is purchased. The tactical option investor is targeting an underlying that he is willing to own if it goes below the strike price of the put, but he also wants exposure to the upside to participate in gains if the underlying makes a large upside move. For example, say we want a long position in the S&P 500. We could purchase one hundred shares of SPY for about $13,400.00. Or we could sell a LEAP put and buy a LEAP call that expires in about one year, January 2012. The 130 put is currently priced at $8.15, and the 135 call is priced at $8.05. This trade would be opened for a net credit of .10, or $10.00 for one contract. The margin requirement would be 20 percent of 130, or $2,600.00. That means that the differ- ence between the cost of the one hundred shares of SPY and the margin requirement for the synthetic long stock position, the $10,800.00, could be invested in a safe, interest-bearing Treasury bond for the duration of the trade. This provides for a better use of capital. If the SPY is below in a year, we'll pur- chase the shares at 130 plus our credit for a net cost of $129.90. Between 130 and 135, we'll keep the $10.00. Above 135 we'll keep the initial credit plus any price above 135. If the S&P has a 10 percent gain for the year, it would close at $147.95. The profit from the synthetic would be $1,305.00, which is a 50 percent gain on the margin requirement, plus the interest on the $10,800.00, which was set aside in a Treasury obligation. With today's low interest rates, the return on the bond is not that much, but in a higher-rate environment, it can add up. If rates were at 5 percent, the return would be $540.00; at 1 percent the return is only $108.00. The key point is that a 10 percent move in the market gave us a 50 percent gain on the margin requirement, and the risk is the same. If you just bought the one hundred shares outright and paid $13,400.00 you'd still have a nice gain of $1,395.00 or 10 percent. Below is a risk-reward graph for a synthetic long stock.

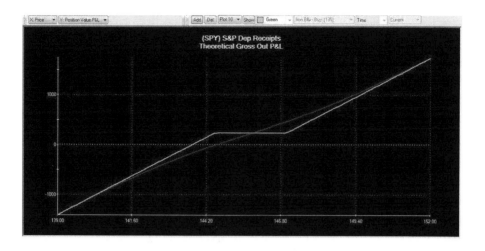

The Long Straddle

I don't believe that traders should have a strategy bias. Traders should study the market and apply the strategy that best applies to their market forecast. Traders with a strategy bias tend to limit their opportunities. However, I do think that it's OK to have a few favorite strategies that you employ when you think that the time is right, and one of my preferred strategies is the long straddle. For those of you unfamiliar with the strategy, the long straddle is the simultaneous purchase of an at-the-money call and put. For example, if XYZ stock is trading at $25, an investor would purchase the 25-strike call and put at the same time. The long straddle is a limited-risk strategy with theoretically unlimited profit potential.

Why purchase a straddle? A straddle should be purchased when the investor forecasts a large price move in the underlying, an increase in implied volatility, or both. It is easier to forecast a move in the implied volatility than to attempt to predict price movement. One of the best times to put on a long straddle is in the weeks preceding a quarterly earnings report. Implied volatilities have a tendency to rise in anticipation of the earnings numbers and peak out just prior to the announcement.

A straddle purchased before the volatility increase can be profitable. Generally straddles should be put on three to four weeks before the announcement so that they can be purchased when the implied volatility is low and appreciate in value as the implied volatility increases as the earnings announcement date approaches.

What are the risks associated with the long straddle? Well, the implied volatility may not increase, and the stock price may remain very stable. In that case, the enemy of the option purchaser, time decay (theta), will take its toll on the position. You may also want to consider the volatility of the broad market before purchasing a straddle. If the broad market has a very high volatility level due to some recent event, it may not be the best time for a straddle. If the VIX is at high levels, you might want to consider another strategy. If the VIX is at normal levels or has declined and the investor is forecasting a rise in the VIX and a rise in the implied volatility of an individual equity due to an impending earnings announcement, a long straddle may be an appropriate strategy.

Is there any way to offset the effects of the time decay as measured by the theta? One tool employed by aggressive traders is known as gamma scalping. When you purchase a straddle, you have the right to buy or sell the underlying at the strike price. So if you are long or short the stock in the same number of shares as your equivalent number of straddle contracts, you have protection against an adverse move in your stock position, regardless of whether you are long or short.

I like to do some scanning to find stocks with a history of implied volatility increase as the earnings date approaches. Then I use a 20-day window and try to locate issues that are trading near a strike price and at a 20-day moving average. I use soft numbers, so the entry can be plus or minus a few cents from either parameter. Then I calculate the daily standard deviation by dividing the annual standard deviation by 16. Why use the number 16? The square root of time is used to calculate standard deviations across multiple time frames. There are 256 trading days in a year. The square root of 256 is 15.87, so that is rounded to 16.

So I have now entered my straddle when the price of the underlying is at a strike and near a moving average. My position is close to being delta neutral. The at-the-money calls and puts should have roughly the same delta. Again I use soft numbers, so I consider a delta of -50 to +50 as being delta neutral. Because I have a long position, it will be gamma positive, so that means that the delta can change rapidly with movement in the underlying and that I will profit from large price swings.

Once the option position is on, if the stock moves up by one standard deviation, I'll short enough shares to make my position delta neutral again. If the stock moves down by one standard deviation, I'll take a long position in the stock. Using round lots, I'll buy enough shares to become delta neutral once again. When the stock returns to its mean, I'll close the position for a small gain. Remember, if the stock moves one standard deviation from its mean, there is a 68 percent probability that it will return to the mean. If it moves two standard deviations, there is a 95 percent chance that it will return to the mean.

By gamma scalping this way, the investor can attempt to earn day-trading profits sufficient to offset the time decay of the position. When things have gone right, I have been able to earn enough day-trading profits from this method to completely cover the cost of the straddle before it is liquidated around the time of the earnings announcement. I don't have a hard rule for exiting the straddle. If profits are adequate from the implied volatility increase, I may liquidate the entire position just before the announcement. On the other hand, I may decide to sell part of the position and keep some through the announcement and try to profit from a large move in the stock. If the position has been paid for by gamma scalping on a daily basis along the way, the investor has a lot of flexibility with his money-management strategy at the exit. As shown in the long straddle profit/loss graph below, the risk is limited to the amount paid for the straddle, and the reward is theoretically unlimited.

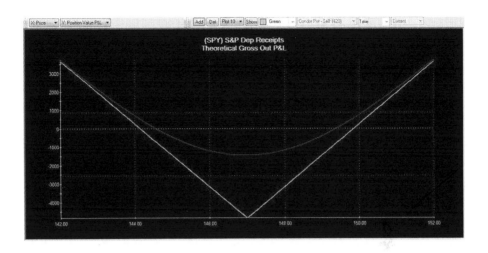

The Collar

The collar consists of a short call and a long put married to a position in an underlying investment. It is especially useful for owners of concentrated equity positions. Say, for example, you are employed at ABC Corporation and are nearing retirement. You've been fortunate enough to accumulate twenty thousand shares of ABC, which is now at $50 per share. The million dollars that you have in ABC is a substantial portion of your net worth. Retirement is two years away, and you can't sleep at night because a decline in the price of ABC could seriously impact your ability to retire. At no cost, you can sell call options on your position and use the proceeds to purchase put options. You can evaluate a wide range of strikes to determine which combination is best for your individual situation. You can sell at-the-money calls and buy at-the-money puts, in which case you are basically locking in the price of ABC and saying that you are content with that price level and are willing to sacrifice further upside gain in order to prevent any loss. You can also use a call spread instead of just a covered call; that way, if the stock makes a large move to the upside, you'll participate in any gain above that highest strike of the spread. You can use it as an income-producing strategy by selling calls slightly out of the money and buying puts further out of the money for a net credit. That way you are retaining some of the call income for your use, and you are setting the maximum downside risk at a predetermined level that you are comfortable with.

Investors who decide to collar an entire position are never happy if the price rises substantially after the collar is put on and they don't participate in that gain. There are a couple of ways to leave some room for upside gain and still have some downside protection. One is simply to collar only a portion of the position. With the twenty thousand shares of ABC, for example, we could decide to only collar ten thousand shares. That would leave ten thousand subject to market risk and ten thousand protected from price decline. The ratio chosen depends on the financial goals and emotional makeup of the investor. The other method for participating in an increase and still having a collar is to use a call spread instead of just a covered call. If ABC is at 50, for example, we could sell the 55 call, buy the 45 put, and buy the 60 calls. If ABC makes a large move, such as a takeover or the development of an exciting new product, we'll participate in the upside gain above $60. When you're using call spreads, ratios can also be employed; the options don't have to be in a one-to-one ratio. For example, with the twenty thousand shares, you could sell two hundred of the 55 calls, buy two hundred of the 45 puts, and buy one hundred of the 60 calls for the upside gain potential. The combinations are virtually limitless, and the ideal combination depends on the investor's unique situation.

If vanilla exchange-trade options don't provide the strike prices and expirations that match your goals, this is an area where using the FLEX options can make a lot of sense. What I do as an RIA is thoroughly evaluate the client's needs and situation, then run calculations on the various option combinations to see what will work best for each investor's unique situation. The proprietary calculations that we use involve solving equations in multiple variables. We'll consider the overall position delta, gamma, and theta. If the investor's goal is to be delta neutral, at the onset we'll sell a 50-delta call and buy a 50-delta put. If the position is put on for a net credit, the delta will work in our favor and provide some income. If it's put on for a net debit, the theta represents the daily expense of maintaining the collar.

Using Call and Put Options to Pay for Stock and ETF Positions

Is anyone a long-term investor anymore? I don't mean people who hold trades for more than fifteen minutes. This is a strategy for investors who identify a stock or ETF that they want to own for several years, then use call and put option selling to generate sufficient cash flow over time to completely pay for the holding. Once the position has been paid for, it can then be held indefinitely.

Here's how it works. The first step is to decide on the stock or ETF that you want to accumulate a long-term position in. I'll leave that up to the reader and focus on explaining how we are going to pay for that position. For the sake of explanation, I am going to use the silver ETF, SLV. This is not a recommendation to purchase SLV; it is merely being used for explanatory purposes.

The strategy consists of three distinct phases. The first phase is the accumulation phase, during which we sell puts and calls until the desired size position is accumulated. The second phase starts once we've accumulated enough shares. Now we just sell calls until we have paid for the cost of the position. The third phase is the holding phase: we have paid for our shares and are holding for long-term capital appreciation. In this writing we'll focus on building the position, not on defending it once it's built or taking profits down the road.

Our hypothetical investor has decided to build a one-thousand-share position in SLV. She starts the process by selling two out-of-the-money front-month SLV puts. Two things can happen here: either the puts will expire worthless, or the SLV will get put to her. If the puts expire worthless, we keep track of the profit earned to pay for the position and repeat the process the next month. If the stock gets put to us, we take delivery of the stock, and we now have two hundred shares. Once we get assigned, we now own two hundred shares, and we will sell two puts and two calls, both out of the money. Now three possible scenarios can unfold. One is that both options expire worthless. In this case we keep track of our profit and repeat until we either get assigned or one goes in the money. The next scenario is that we get assigned another two hundred shares and the call expires worthless. Now we will own four hundred shares, and we'll repeat the process again next month. Third, if the call goes into the money prior to expiration, since we want to accumulate shares, not liquidate them, we'll roll those calls for a credit into the next expiration.

Once we've met our goal for accumulation, one thousand shares, by repeating the process of selling puts and calls, we'll stop selling the puts and just sell calls until we have collected sufficient premium to pay for the total cost of the position. Then our purchase price for the position has been returned to us, and we can hold that investment as long as we wish.

Looking at actual prices of SLV as of this writing, selling the first strike out of the money on the calls and puts would generate $1.70. SLV is trading at $26.10 ($1.70 is 6.5 percent of the price of SLV). If you could collect that much premium each month, it would only take sixteen months to pay off the position if the price remained static, which it won't. If the price were static, you wouldn't get any option premium; volatility is a factor that helps determine the option price. Volatile stocks will have higher premiums than less volatile stocks. Because prices are obviously not static, it's impossible to determine in advance how long it will take to build and pay off your position, but a good rule of thumb for an issue with good option premiums should be two to three years. Hypothetically, say you already owned one thousand shares of SLV and that your cost was $26.00 per share. The next month's first-strike out-of-the-money calls are at $0.72. If you could collect that much each month just from the calls, it would take thirty-six months, or three years, to pay off your position.

The reality of building positions this way is that some months you'll have stock getting put to you, some months you'll be rolling calls up and out for a credit, and some months both sides will expire worthless and you'll keep the credit. You'll need to keep track of every trade, including the costs, and keep with the strategy until your stock is accumulated.

Advanced Call-Writing Strategies
Delta-Neutral Call Writing

Much has been written about the popular covered call writing strategy, in which an investor will purchase one hundred shares of a stock or an ETF and sell one call option for some income and partial downside protection. The term *covered call* means that for every option you sell, that option contract is covered by one hundred shares of the underlying investment.

Advanced option traders will be familiar with the term *delta neutral*. For those readers who are not familiar, the term means that your position has no market directional bias. In other words, the position is neutral to market movement. If we buy one hundred shares of XYZ stock, that position alone will have a delta of 100. Now, if we sell an at-the-money call with a delta of 50, because we are short the call, it will have a negative delta, so the net position delta will be 50 (100 deltas for the one hundred shares of XYZ stock and -50 deltas for the short XYZ call). This is how your typical covered call position works. If you were to sell an out-of-the-money call with a delta of 25, your net position delta would be 75. In other words, the total position would behave like 75 shares of the underlying instead of 100.

Now, if we want to create a market-neutral position, we'll sell enough calls so that the net position is delta neutral. So if we buy one hundred shares of XYZ again, we could sell two 50-delta at-the-money calls, three 33-delta out-of-the-money calls, or four 25-delta out-of-the-money calls, and so on. If the net position delta is at or near 0, your position will not have directional risk as long as it remains delta neutral. Then you can earn the theta, or the decay, from the short options. You don't have to sell the options at just one strike price, either. For example, you could sell one at-the-money 50-delta call and two out-of-the-money 25-delta calls.

Once a position is established, the delta will change by the rate of the gamma, and adjustments will have to be made to remain delta neutral. You can adjust the shares of stock you own, sell more calls, or buy some calls back to make the adjustment.

As with any strategy, there are risks. The underlying can drop rapidly before you can adjust, and you can experience a loss. Since you have uncovered short calls, if the underlying explodes upward rapidly, you can also experience a substantial loss. Stocks that have high volatility or may be potential takeover targets should be avoided. Megacap stocks or broad-based index ETFs can be good candidates for a delta-neutral strategy. Indexes can rise and fall rapidly, but they cannot drop all the way to zero the way individual equities can or explode upward the way stocks getting taken over can.

Looking at some current prices as of this writing, the SPY is at $131.82, and the Feb 135 calls are twenty-one days from expiration. The Feb 135 calls sell for $0.61 and have a delta of 24. You could sell four of those calls against a one-hundred-share position of SPY and take in $2.44 in premium; the theta is -0.03, so you'd be getting $12.00 per day in decay. You could regularly make delta-neutral adjustments as time went on, but you wouldn't have to worry about loss unless the SPY rose to above 135 by expiration. This is not a recommendation for the above SPY trade; I just like using real numbers to illustrate.

Synthetic Option Positions
One of the advantages of trading options is their virtually unlimited flexibility. For any strategy or position considered, there are virtually unlimited possibilities. If one is to consider

all the different strike prices and expirations to choose from, the universe is huge. Now consider for a moment that for every option position, there exists a synthetic equivalent.

Say, for example, that you are considering purchasing a long call. Hypothetically, there are ten strikes for that option and also ten different expirations that could be used. That means that there are one hundred different call options to evaluate to see what fits your market prognosis the best.

Now consider that there is also a synthetic equivalent to a long call. The equivalent is long stock plus a long put. There is only one long stock position to consider, but hypothetically assume that there are also ten strikes and ten expirations to consider for the long put. That means that in addition to the one hundred call options to evaluate, you can also evaluate one hundred long put positions to combine with the long stock. So now you have two hundred different positions to consider.

That's the beauty of using options: the possibilities are virtually unlimited, and there is no limit to the amount of creative thinking that can be applied.

Remember, for each position, there exists a synthetic equivalent. Here's a table of the basic ones.

Long Stock = Long Call + Short Put
Short Put = Long Stock + Short Call
Long Put = Short Stock + Long Call
Long Call = Long Stock + Long Put
Short Call = Short Stock + Short Put
Short Stock = Long Put + Short Call

Since there are many complex option strategies to use, it makes sense that a synthetic equivalent could be used for any of the legs of a normal option strategy if it is advantageous.

Dynamic Delta Hedging
Dynamic delta hedging is a term used for adjusting the delta of an option position due to price changes in the

underlying security. One of the beauties and challenges of options trading is that there are so many different combinations to consider for any market outlook. Say you're an income-oriented investor and you have just established a delta-neutral iron condor. In order to receive the maximum profit, you want the underlying security to stay between the two strikes and the entire position to expire worthless. As the stock or ETF begins to move, your position will start taking on delta. The gamma of your position is the rate of change of the delta. If you were delta neutral when the position was initiated, check your gamma; that is, how much will the delta move with a one-point move in the underlying? By knowing the gamma, you can be prepared to make adjustments to your position to remain delta neutral. Complex positions that have a high positive theta will also have short gamma, meaning that you have to be prepared to adjust according to price movement in the underlying. In the case of a delta-neutral iron condor, if the underlying makes an upward price move, you have the choice of adding some long calls, more short puts, or some long shares of the underlying stock. If it makes a downward move, you can add long puts or short calls or short some of the stock. Instead of just adding, you can also look to reduce some contracts: in the case of an upward move, you'd want to buy back some of the short calls; in the case of a downward move, you could buy back some of the short puts, or you could consider any combination of the above.

One thing you need to consider is how often you want to adjust. Do want to check your position once daily or several times during the trading day? Another consideration is how you choose to define *delta neutral*. Of course the strict definition is that *delta neutral* means zero deltas; however, when it comes to trading, you should establish a guideline so that you'll allow some flexibility. It's impossible to stay at exactly zero, so a good rule of thumb might be to say that you'll allow a range of plus or minus 50 deltas. Then allow the position to range from -50 deltas to +50 deltas, and don't make any adjustments until those levels are exceeded.

The final consideration is how to make the adjustments, and that is where the fun comes in. Because there are so many different possibilities to evaluate for each position, it is wisest to use an expected return calculator to see which adjustments have the best mathematical expectancy. Remember, if you want to add delta and want to add to the position, you can buy stock, buy calls, or sell puts. If you want to subtract delta and want to add to the position, you can buy puts, sell calls, or short stock. You can also adjust delta by closing out part of the existing position. Evaluating all of the possibilities is what makes options trading so flexible and challenging.

Put-Call Parity

Put-call parity is an important concept for options traders to understand. What it means is that the price of a put option and the price of a call option are such that no risk-free arbitrage opportunity exists to create profitable conversions or reversals. A conversion consists of a long put, a long stock, and a short call, while a reversal, or reverse conversion, is the exact opposite: short stock, short put, and long call. The formula for put-call parity is as follows:

$$C(t) - P(t) = S(t) - K \times B(t, T)$$

C (t) is the value of the call at time t
P (t) is the put value at time t
S (t) is the stock price
K is the strike price
B (t, T) is the value of a bond that matures at time T

The math is very simple. The reality of the marketplace is such that you won't be able to find profitable conversions and reversals because the arbitrage opportunities don't exist. If they do, they quickly disappear.

Expected Return

The concept of expected return is critical for options traders to understand. The expected return is known as the weighted average outcome. The math is really simple and can be shown as follows: say you were considering an investment that had a 25 percent chance of a 20 percent return, a 25 percent chance of a 10 percent return, a 25 percent chance of a 5 percent return, and a 25 percent chance of a -5 percent return. The formula would look like this:

Expected Return = (0.25) (0.2) + (0.25) (0.1) + (0.25) (0.05) + (0.25) (-0.05) = 7.5%

If you are an options trader or if you use options to reduce risk and enhance return on your investment portfolio, you need to get in the habit of using an option calculator to calculate the expected return on any position you are considering. Options without an expected profit should not be used. Scan the market for strategies that have a positive expected return.

Say, for example, someone challenges you to a game of coin toss. You can pick heads or tails, and you can play as long as you wish. If the payout was the same for either heads or tails, say one dollar, there would be no statistical advantage to the game and no reason to play. Now if you were the receive two dollars when you won and only had to pay one dollar when you lost, you'd have a huge statistical advantage—and a reason to play as much as possible.

Casino games are like the above example, but the casino gets $1.05 when it wins, and you get $0.095. When trading options, use an expected return calculator, find trades where the expected return is on your side, and always manage your risk.

Chapter Six:

EXCHANGE-TRADED FUND EXPLOSION

Since the first ETF came onto the market, there has been an explosion in the number and variety of ETFs available for purchase. ETFs provide a real advantage to investors because they are very simple to trade, most have low expense ratios, and they can give an investor the ability to diversify like never before. The difference between an exchange-traded fund and a traditional open-end fund is that the ETF trades throughout the trading day on an exchange. An open-end fund only trades at the price at the end of the day. If an investor purchases shares in an open-end fund, the fund will create new shares for that purchase. If an investor liquidates fund holdings, the transaction occurs at the end-of-the-day price, and the fund can decrease the total number of shares. The transaction goes through at the net asset value, or NAV, of the fund. One disadvantage of the open-end fund is that the fund can decline quite a bit in one day from the time the investor makes the sell decision to the time that decision is executed. With an ETF, the investor gets the current price without having to wait until the end of the day. With very small amounts of money, investors can diversify into various markets, including equity indexes, fixed-income indexes, commodities, and currencies. Today over one-fourth of all equity trades are done with ETFs, and the four equities with the highest trading volume are ETFs.

Currently there are about nine hundred ETFs on the market. Of those, some are optionable, and some are not. Of the ones that are optionable, some do not have sufficient liquidity to trade well. I like to focus on those options that have high option volume and very tight spreads, preferably the penny pilot issues. We'll have a brief discussion of some of the most liquid ETFs and ones that can be used to construct a highly diversified portfolio.

There are ETFs on broad-based indexes, sectors, fixed income, commodities, currencies, foreign countries, and more. For now, for the equity ETFs, we'll focus on the broad-based indexes. A highly diversified portfolio that does not have company- or sector-specific risk can be constructed using the broad-based indexes. Many of the popular indexes have more than one fund that tracks them. For the purpose of this discourse, if the index, currency, or commodity has multiple symbols, we'll look at the symbol that has the highest option liquidity. If you plan to incorporate an option strategy into your portfolio management, you have to stick with the most liquid ETFs that also have a very liquid options market. Many of the popular ETFs are penny pilot issues and are on the weekly expiration cycle. Sticking with these funds will give you a lot more flexibility when designing and applying your option strategies. You may want to consider ETFs that are not as liquid if they will provide diversification to your portfolio. Some of the commodity-based funds—like KOL, which is coal—can help diversify your portfolio, and the options have adequate liquidity even though they are not nearly as liquid as the options on the SPY, for example.

There are other factors to be considered when purchasing an ETF. The expense ratio is one, but you also have to look at the total expenses, including trading costs and tracking error. Tracking error is the difference between the fund's actual performance and the performance of the underlying index. Many of the major brokerages now offer commission-free ETF trading for certain funds, so you should check with your broker to see which funds are eligible for commission-free trading. Fidelity and TD Ameritrade had a pretty good lineup of commission-free ETFs as of this writing.

Inverse and Leveraged ETFs

There are also now ETFs that are inverse and are also leveraged. An example of a leveraged ETF is the SSO, which is designed to have twice the daily movement of the S&P 500. The SDS is an inverse S&P 500 fund, so it will increase in value as the S&P 500 declines. The inverse and leveraged ETFs give the tactical option investor an extra tool to employ. For example, if an investor wishes to hedge a portfolio that is highly correlated to the S&P 500 instead of buying puts on the SPY, now he can buy calls on the SDS and achieve the same effect. Which is better depends on a variety of factors, including the pricing of the options considered. When purchasing puts or calls, tactical investors always pay attention to the implied volatility and the theta, or the rate of decay. Inverse ETFs have opened up more possibilities for hedgers and investors. The following diagram illustrates some of the possibilities based on market opinion.

Bullish	Bearish
SPY Strategies: Volatility-VXX	**SPY Strategies:** Volatility-VXX
• Long SPY	• Short SPY
• Long SPY Calls	• Long SPY Puts
• Long SSO	• Short SSO
• Long SSO Calls	• Long SSO Puts
• Short VXX	• Long VXX
• Long VXX Puts	• Long VXX Calls
• Short SDS	• Long SDS
• Long SDS Puts	• Long SDS Calls
• Long VIX Puts	• Long VIX Calls
• SPXU Short	• SPXU Long
• Short SH	• Long SH
• Long UPRO	• Short UPRO
IWM Strategies: Volatility-RVX	**IWM Strategies:** Volatility-RVX
• Short RWM	• Long RWM
• Long RWM Puts	• Long RWM Calls
• Short TWM	• Long TWM
• Long TWM Puts	• Long TWM Calls
• Long UWM	• Short UWM
• Long UWM Calls	• Long UWM Puts
• Long IWM Calls	• Long IWM Puts
• Long IWM	• Short IWM
EEM Strategies:	**EEM Strategies:**
• Short EUM	• Long EUM
• Short EEV	• Long EEV
• Long EEV Puts	• Long EEV Calls
• Long EET	• Short EET
• Long EET Calls	• Long EET Puts
• Long EEM Calls	• Long EEM Puts
• Long EEM	• Short EEM

Bullish	Bearish
EFA Strategies: • Short EFZ • Short EFU • Long EFO • Long EFA Calls • Long EFA	**EFA Strategies:** • Long EFZ • Long EFU • Short EFO • Long EFA Calls • Short EFA
GLD Strategies: Volatility-GVZ • Short GLL • Long GLL Puts • Long UGL • Long UGL Calls • Long GLD Calls • Long GLD	**GLD Strategies:** Volatility-GVZ • Long GLL • Long GLL Calls • Short UGL • Long UGL Puts • Long GLD Puts • Short GLD
USO Strategies: Volatility-OVX • Short SCO • Long SCO Puts • Long UCO • Long UCO Calls • Long USO Calls • Long USO	**USO Strategies:** Volatility-GVZ • Long SCO • Long SCO Calls • Short UCO • Long UCO Puts • Long USO Puts • Short USO

Understanding Leveraged and Inverse Funds

You may have heard about funds that will deliver twice or even three times the performance of an index. There are also funds that are inverse an index or double and even triple inverse. The SPY is the ETF that tracks the S&P 500, which is a stock index made up of 500 of the largest companies in the United States. An example of a leveraged ETF is the SSO, which is designed to have twice the daily movement of the S&P 500. There is also a short fund for the SPY called the SH; it will go up when the SPY declines. The SDS is a leveraged inverse S&P

500 fund, so it will increase in value by twice the amount the S&P declines on a daily basis.

Leveraged and inverse funds are relatively new and can be good tools for portfolio management. Prior to having the inverse funds available, if an investor wanted to hedge a portfolio that had a high correlation to the S&P 500, he would have had to buy puts on the S&P 500 or short a futures contract. Today an investor can simply buy shares of the SH or the SDS.

However, along with these benefits come added risks. Before purchasing a leveraged or inverse fund, it is critically important to understand its structure. The funds are designed to move up by twice the amount of an index, move up if an index declines, or move up double or triple the amount an index declines on a daily basis. The key word here is *daily*. Over longer time periods, these funds will not perform with double leverage. Due to what's known as "roll costs" and daily market volatility, the funds may not perform well over longer time periods.

You can own a leveraged index fund, watch the index gain over a long time period, but see the leveraged fund decline in value. Here's a real-world example as reported by the Securities and Exchange Commission (SEC). Between December 1, 2008, and April 30, 2009, a certain index gained 2 percent. A leveraged fund that delivered twice the daily performance fell by 6 percent. During the same time frame, an ETF seeking to deliver three times the daily performance of an index fell by 53 percent, while the underlying index gained about 8 percent. Read the prospectus and use caution when considering leveraged or inverse funds.

Following are brief descriptions of a few of the most liquid exchange-traded funds.

Spyder (SPY)

Spyder is the granddaddy of the ETF world. Spyder is a fund that represents the Standard and Poor's 500 Index, the S&P 500. It has very high liquidity and has penny pilot and dollar strike options. It also has a large number of expiration cycles, including long-term LEAPS, quarterly, monthly, and now weekly issues. The weekly issues create some great opportunities for income-oriented investors. For example, say an investor is going to write covered calls on a SPY holding. The investor does not want to write a monthly call because there is an event scheduled two weeks away that the investor believes could impact the price of the S&P 500, like a normally scheduled meeting of the Federal Reserve Board. The investor now can sell a weekly option that will expire prior to the meeting and wait for the meeting results to write the next option. The SPY pays a quarterly dividend.

Diamond (DIA)

The DIA represents the thirty stocks that comprise the Dow Jones Industrial Average. The DIA pays a reasonable dividend, currently over 3 percent. It is also very liquid and is a penny pilot issue with dollar strikes and LEAPS, and quarterly, monthly, and weekly expiration dates.

Nasdaq 100 (QQQ)

The Nasdaq 100 Index ETF is known as the Qs. The options have similar liquidity and expiration cycles to the SPY and DIA.

Russell 2000 (IWM)

The Russell 2000 Index ETF represents small-cap stocks and has similar liquidity and expiration cycles to the ETFs above.

Emerging Markets (EEM)

The EEM ETF correlates to the Emerging Markets Index. The liquidity and expiration cycles are similar to the US-based indexes discussed above. The EEM pays an annual dividend.

EAFE (EFA)

The EAFE Index is the index for Europe, Asia, and the Far East. It represents foreign-developed equities. Again the liquidity and expiration cycles are similar to the equity indexes discussed above. The dividend is paid annually.

Long-Term Treasury Bond (TLT)

The maturities for the Long-Term Treasury Bond Index are over twenty years. The TLT fund pays a monthly dividend. The TLT options are penny pilot, have LEAPS and monthly and weekly expirations, and trade in dollar strikes, but they are not quite as liquid as SPY and can have wider spreads. Modern portfolio theory suggests that adding bonds to an equity portfolio provides diversification and lowers risk. Bonds can have a low or even negative correlation to equities. The primary risk in a long-term bond fund is interest-rate risk. Long-term bond funds can decline in value during a rising-interest-rate environment.

Intermediate-Term Treasury Bond Fund (IEF)

The maturities of the bonds in the Intermediate-Term Treasury Bond Fund range from seven to ten years. It also pays a monthly dividend. IEF has a very low statistical volatility, so the option premiums are not very high but can potentially enhance the return on an IEF holding. The options are less liquid than TLT, so the spreads are even wider. They also do not have as many expiration dates as TLT; currently there are no weekly options available for the IEF.

Gold (GLD)

The gold fund buys and stores physical gold in warehouses, so there is some expense involved. Gold can be a great diversifier to an equity portfolio. GLD has options that have very high liquidity, trade in dollar increments, and are penny pilot issues. GLD also has numerous expiration cycles, including LEAPS, monthly issues, and the new weekly issues.

Silver (SLV)

The silver fund owns and stores physical bars of silver. Silver is another powerful diversification tool for an equity-based portfolio. SLV options are also highly liquid, have dollar strikes and penny pilot pricing, and have expiration cycles similar to GLD.

Oil (USO)

Oil can be a good diversifier, but the price is very volatile and sensitive to economic conditions. USO options have very high liquidity, including dollar strikes and penny pilot pricing, and have numerous expirations with LEAPS, monthly options, and weekly options.

Coal (KOL)

The Market Vectors Coal ETF holds coal. KOL can be another good diversifier to an equity portfolio. KOL options have decent liquidity but have wider spreads than the more liquid ETFs like the SPY. KOL is not a penny pilot issue. It does have dollar strikes but does not have the LEAPS or the new weekly options.

Japanese Yen (FXY)

Currently the Japanese yen is considered a risk-adverse asset, so it can be another good diversification tool for a portfolio that consists primarily of equity indexes. The FXY options have dollar strikes and LEAPS but do not have weekly options or penny pilot pricing, so the spreads will be wider.

Volatility Index

A recent development has been the creation of ETFs on the VIX. There is one for short-term and one for longer-term. The symbols are VXX for the short-term and VXZ for the long-term. VXX is a blended average of the front two VIX futures months. VXZ is a blended average of months four through seven. The VXX is much more liquid than the VXZ. Both have options; they are not penny pilot issues. The VXX has just recently begun trading the weekly expirations.

Numerous studies have been done on using the VIX to hedge equity portfolios. Goldman Sachs did one that concluded that VIX options could be a very effective portfolio management tool for risk reduction.

If you're going to consider using the VIX as a hedge, it's important to understand what the VIX is and how it works. The VIX is a mathematical calculation that is derived from the implied volatilities of at- and near-the-money options on the S&P 500. The original VIX was based on the OEX 100 and was introduced in 1993. The current VIX was introduced in 2003. It has a different derivation and is calculated from the S&P 500. If the implied volatilities are high, the VIX will be higher. If implied volatilities are low, the VIX will have a low reading. In 2004 futures were introduced on the VIX, and options were added in 2006.

The VIX is also called "the fear index." When there is a great deal of uncertainty in the market and times are turbulent, the VIX will have a high reading. When markets are strong and investors are bullish and complacent, the VIX will have a low reading. It also has a tendency to have a reasonably well-defined range. Unlike a stock, it can't go to zero and won't tend to trend in only one direction for long periods of time. It will tend to range from low to high along with market conditions. One characteristic of volatility is that it tends to manifest itself in clusters rather than random patterns.

So how can an individual investor use the VIX for portfolio protection? Not too long ago, an investor would have had to buy and roll call options on the VIX index. This process worked well, but one had to consider the time decay of the options and the term structure. VIX options are based on the VIX futures, so each month's option series correlates to that month's futures contract. Some months may be priced higher or lower than others, depending on the outlook of market participants. A strategy of rolling call options could be difficult for individual investors to implement effectively.

Today an investor who wants a hedge and who doesn't want a short position or an option position with time decay can purchase shares of the VXX. This is best done when it is near the low end of its historical trading range. Avoid purchasing VXX shares when it's near the high end of its range even if you think it's going higher. When it is closer to the high end of the historical trading range, the risks of purchasing at that level are too high. The market can rally, and the VXX can drop in value very rapidly. If the VXX is already at a high level and you have the opinion that it is going higher or need to hedge by using it, you should buy call options instead of the underlying; this will limit your risk while still allowing you the ability to participate in any upside gain. The VXX can be held indefinitely, just like a mutual fund. Once the VXX position has been purchased, it is held until something happens to the market to increase the volatility. If the market gets spooked by bad earnings reports, poor economic data, or unforeseen global events like natural disasters, war, terrorist attacks, and the like, the VIX will spike, and profits can be realized from the VXX position; these profits can help to offset declines in a long-term portfolio or be used as a stand-alone trade.

VXX can also be used as a hedge and as an income-producing covered call writing investment. The options on the VXX are reasonably liquid and have dollar strikes, but they are now penny pilot issues. They have LEAPS, and now the weekly issues are trading.

The Difference between an ETF and an ETN

The last few years have seen an explosion in the number of ETFs on the market. The very first ETF was launched in Canada in 1989; it tracked the Toronto 35 Index. The first ETF in the United States was the Spyder, which tracks the S&P 500 Index. It was launched in 1993 along with the Diamond, which tracks the Dow Jones Industrial Average. By 2002 there were over two hundred ETFs trading, and today the number is over a thousand.

With an ETF the investor is exposed to market risk because the ETF will track an underlying index and is also exposed to a type of risk known as tracking error. Tracking error means that the performance of the ETF may not match its underlying index exactly. The Spyder tracks the S&P 500 but can vary slightly due to trading costs and other expenses. The Spyder holds the stocks that make up the S&P 500, so if an investor decides to sell, he'll get the price of the Spyder at that time, which will be very close to the value of the S&P 500.

In recent years, along with the ETF explosion, there has been a new type of exchange-traded fund, known as an exchange-traded note, or ETN. One advantage of ETNs is that they can reduce or eliminate tracking error. But they also carry an additional risk that ETFs don't have, and that is credit risk.

ETNs are issued with maturity dates as senior debt notes by the bank; as a consequence, they carry credit risk like bonds. The investor in an ETN receives a promise to be repaid by the issuing bank. So even though the ETN may track a stock index, its price can be influenced by the credit rating of the issuing bank. Barclay's Bank was the first issuer of ETNs and is the largest participant in the market. Barclay's has an AA credit rating, is over three hundred years old, and has $1.5 trillion in assets. Its reputation is solid, but an ETN investor is still exposed to the risk of the bank failing. Barings Bank was another large bank with a great reputation, having financed the Napoleonic Wars. Barings failed because of the actions of one rogue trader.

ETNs can be useful investment products, but investors need to be aware of the additional risks they pose and use them appropriately.

Chapter Seven:

MODEL PORTFOLIOS

The *Option Advisor* newsletter provides all of the information needed for an individual to take control of his or her own investments. Detailed information is given on how to construct and manage three different model portfolios designed to produce income, with risk controls in mind at all times.

ETF Covered Call Model

The objective of the ETF covered call portfolio is to provide total return from a highly diversified ETF portfolio with relatively low volatility. Call options are written monthly to provide cash flow. Subscribers to the *Option Advisor* newsletter get the information needed to manage the covered call ETF model portfolio on their own. Investors can purchase the underlying ETFs or stocks and sell the call options, or as an alternative they can sell cash-secured puts and not sell the calls until they get assigned on the puts. Then they go through a cycle of getting called and selling the puts until assignment occurs.

The portfolio will hold ETFs on the world's major stock market indexes and US Treasury bonds and will add currencies and commodities if they add diversification to the portfolio. Currencies and commodities may be added based on fundamental research, relative-strength analysis, correlation analysis, and a screen for option liquidity. The portfolio turnover can be high and is well suited for qualified accounts or for investors for whom a high-turnover portfolio is suitable.

The ETF universe is monitored to locate funds that have sufficient option liquidity and provide diversification to the model. Correlation analysis is used to determine the optimal fund mix. Portfolio volatility is reduced by holding assets with low correlation and by selling call options. Company-specific risk, also known as nonsystematic risk, is completely eliminated by the use of index-based ETFs. The typical composition of the portfolio will be a mix of equity, debt, currency, and commodity funds.

Once the fund allocation has been determined, call options are written monthly. To determine which options to write, we use an option-pricing model and evaluate the theta, delta, gamma, vega, and implied volatility of the available strike prices and choose options that will contribute the most to the portfolio in terms of total return. A $200,000 portfolio will typically have a theta of about $100 per day, which means that if the underlying funds were to stay flat and produce no return, the investor would receive $100 per day just from option decay.

In addition to more traditional option-pricing models like Black-Scholes, we also use a generalized autoregressive conditional heteroskedasticity (GARCH) model to study the conditional variance of the returns of the ETFs. One of the consequences of dependency in asset returns is that the volatility of these returns tends to exhibit patterns. Volatility is not random but has a tendency to appear in clusters, and these clusters have a tendency to be persistent over time. While periods of high volatility tend to be a concern for most investors, we look forward to the higher option premiums and enhanced income produced during those times. We have found that the Black-Scholes model will tend to underprice options during periods of high volatility and overprice them during periods of low volatility. Volatility forecasting helps us to determine which call options to sell.

Currently the model holds the SPY, IWM, DIA, EEM, EFA, TLT, IEF, GLD, SLV, FXF, MOO, and UNG. New funds may be added as more ETFs become available and become optionable with sufficient liquidity.

The screening process consists of monitoring the ETF universe for new issues to see which issues become optionable. If they are optionable, they must have sufficient option liquidity to sell large numbers of contracts and have tight bid-ask spreads. Funds may be added if they'll provide diversification to a portfolio consisting of the world's major stock market indices. If the funds meet those criteria, they are then analyzed from a fundamental and technical perspective to determine whether they are suitable candidates for purchase.

The theoretical basis for the model comes from several different major academic studies. While most investors have heard of the random-walk theory and the efficient-markets hypothesis, known as EMH, the question of how to apply those theories to individual portfolio management can present some problems. Random walkers believe that they should stay fully invested in low-cost index funds for the long haul. The EMH theory states that markets are efficient, that all information is already built in to the current price, and that movement cannot be predicted. Recent years have given us great advancement in the field of behavioral finance, which tells us that investors are not rational all the time. The adaptive markets hypothesis, or AMH, attempts to reconcile the differences between EMH and behavioral finance. While academics continue to research and debate, investors have a need to produce income, get acceptable returns, and have comfortable risk levels. We follow the most recent developments in the academic world to determine whether newly available research can help us enhance portfolio return and reduce risk or portfolio volatility.

The covered call income model benefits from combining elements of different widely accepted studies. The portfolio holds low-cost equity index funds as the EMH and random walkers suggest. We produce income from those funds by selling call options.

Modern portfolio theory, or MPT, was developed by Harry Markowitz, who won a Nobel Prize in economics for his work. The theory says that by combining assets classes with low correlation, an investor can get better returns and lower risk. The covered call model follows MPT by being broadly diversified across major asset classes.

Dr. John Lintner of Harvard University was one of the original developers of the capital asset pricing model, or CAPM. In 1983 he wrote a paper showing that using commodity futures in a traditional stock-and-bond portfolio enhanced return and lowered risk. The covered call model will add low-cost commodity ETFs to lower risk by providing greater diversification than can be found in a traditional stock-and-bond portfolio.

There have been a few major studies that also show that a buy-write strategy on an equity index will deliver superior risk-adjusted returns. In 2007 Kapadia and Szado at the Isenberg School of Management at the University of Massachusetts did a study on writing calls on the Russell 2000 Index that concluded, "The results demonstrate that the strategy has consistently outperformed the Russell 2000 Index on a risk adjusted basis." There is further evidence that call writing can lower risk: in 2006 Callan Associates did a similar evaluation of a buy-write strategy on the S&P 500 Index and concluded that the covered call strategy delivered superior risk-adjusted returns over an eighteen-year period from 1988 to 2006. The covered call model includes both the S&P 500 and the Russell 2000 Index in the portfolio.

Robert Engle won the Nobel Prize in economics in 2003 "for methods of analyzing economic time series with time varying volatility (ARCH)." ARCH and GARCH models as mentioned above can be useful tools for forecasting volatility. We employ volatility forecasting to determine which option strikes to write for our covered call model.

The proprietary methodology used to manage the covered call income model is based on the results of our own research, which has a solid foundation based on numerous widely accepted academic studies.

The model returns are as follows:	
2006	9.71%
2007	11.06%
2008	-5.15%
2009	12.18%
2010	9.44%
2011	2.77%
2012	3.17%

These returns were generated with a very low volatility—a standard deviation of 6.64—which is less than half the standard deviation of the stock market.

Blue-Chip Covered Call Dividend Model

The blue-chip covered call dividend model is an income solution for investors seeking cash flow who want an alternative to today's record-low bond yields. The portfolio consists of high-dividend-paying blue-chip stocks. The stocks selected have a dividend yield of at least 3 percent, and all of the stocks are on the penny pilot program. These stocks are also components of the major indexes, like the Dow and the S&P 500. The screening process for the underlying stocks is a combination of dividend yield, fundamental ratings, and technical analysis. Technical analysis is not relied on too much, but, for example, if we have a stock that has strong fundamentals and a good dividend, but we look at a price chart and the share price is breaking down, we may choose to avoid that issue until the price stabilizes.

In addition to collecting the dividends and gains from these stocks, we sell call options every month that are approximately

2 percent out of the money. The combination of dividends and option premium gives this portfolio a very strong cash flow. Conservative investors can also purchase puts for protection. This will limit downside risk, such as loss due to a market meltdown or an individual stock blowing up. In this case we sell call options that are about 2 percent out of the money each month, but about six months out, we also buy put options that are about 8 percent out of the money.

Kapadia and Szado did a study and concluded that writing calls 2 percent out of the money each month and buying puts 8 percent out of the money every six months yielded the best results. The blue-chip covered call model returned 12.98 percent in 2011 and 15.45 percent in 2012. With the put protection in place, the returns were lower by about 3 percent each year, but investors had peace of mind knowing that they had some protection in place in the event of a major market selloff.

Aggressive High Dividend + Covered Call Model

Newsletter subscribers also get the trades to manage a portfolio of very high dividend stocks and instructions on how to sell covered calls on them. These stocks all have very high dividend yields of over 6 percent but are not penny pilot issues and are not as liquid as the stocks in the blue-chip model. Because these stocks trade thinner, there can be wide bid-ask spreads. We sell options on these stocks quarterly or even semiannually due to the liquidity constraints. Due to the wide spreads, the sell orders are usually placed about midway between the bid and the ask, and investors sometimes have to wait patiently to get their trades filled. The additional income from selling the call options increases the overall portfolio return and gives some downside risk protection. This portfolio has been generating in excess of 10 percent return from the combination of dividends, capital gains, and option premium.

Appendix:

LIST OF PENNY PILOT STOCKS AND ETFS

UNDERLYING SYMBOL	UNDERLYING NAME
A	Agilent Technologies
AA	Alcoa
AAPL	Apple
ABKFQ	Ambac
ABT	Abbot Labs
ABX	Barrick Gold
ACAS	American Capital
ACI	Arch Coal
ADBE	Adobe Systems
ADM	Archer Daniels Midland
ADSK	Autodesk
AEM	Agnico-Eagle Mines
AET	Aetna
AFL	Aflac
AGO	Assured Guaranty
AIG	American International Group
AKAM	Akamai
AKS	AK Steel
ALL	Allstate
AMAT	Applied Materials
AMD	Advanced Micro Devices
AMED	Amedisys
AMGN	Amgen

AMLN	Amylin
AMR	AMR Corp
AMZN	Amazon
ANF	Abercrombie and Fitch
ANR	Alpha Natural Resources
APA	Apache
APC	Anadarko Petroleum
APOL	Apollo Group
APWR	A-Power Energy
ARNA	Arena Pharmaceuticals
ATPG	ATP Oil and Gas
ATVI	Activision
AUY	Yamana Gold
AXP	American Express
BA	Boeing
BAC	Bank of America
BAX	Baxter
BBBY	Bed Bath and Beyond
BBD	Banco Bradesco
BBT	BB&T
BBY	Best Buy
BCRX	Biocrest Pharmecueticals
BHI	Baker Hughes
BHP	BHP Billiton
BIDU	Baidu
BK	Bank of New York Mellon
BMY	Bristol Meyers
BP	British Petroleum
BPOP	Popular
BRCD	Brocade
BRCM	Broadcom
BRK/B	Berkshire Hathaway
BSX	Boston Scientific
BSZ	CBOE S&P 500 Index Binary Options
BTU	Peabody Energy
BUCY	Bucyrus

BVZ	CBOE Volatility Index Binary Options
BX	Blackstone Group
C	Citigroup
CAT	Caterpillar
CB	Chubb
CBO	Siac
CELG	Celgene
CENX	Century Aluminum
CF	CF Industries
CHK	Chesapeake
CI	Cigna
CIEN	Ciena
CIT	CIT Group
CL	Colgate Palmolive
CLF	Cliffs Natural Resources
CMA	Comerica
CMCSA	Comcast
CNX	Consol Energy
COF	Capital One
COP	Conoco Phillips
COST	Costco
CREE	Cree
CRM	Salesforce
CSCO	Cisco
CSX	CSX
CTIC	Cell Therapeutics
CVS	CVS Caremark
CVX	Chevron
CX	Cemex
DAL	Delta Air Lines
DCTH	Delcath Systems
DD	Dupont
DE	Deere
DELL	Dell
DHI	DR Horton
DIA	Spyder Dow Jones Ind Av ETF Trust

DIS	Walt Disney
DJX	Dow Jones Industrial Average Index
DNDN	Dendreon
DO	Diamond Offshore
DOW	Dow Chemical
DRYS	Dryships
DTV	Direct TV
DVN	Devon Energy
EBAY	Ebay
EEM	IShares MSCI Emerging Markets Index
EFA	IShares MSCI EAFE Index
EK	Eastman Kodak
EMC	EMC
ENER	Energy Conversion Devices
EOG	EOG Resources
EP	El Paso
ERTS	Electronic Arts
ESI	ITT Educational
ESRX	Express Scripts
ETFC	Etrade
EWJ	IShares MSCI Japan
EWT	IShares MSCI Taiwan
EWW	IShares MSCI Mexico
EWY	IShares MSCI South Korea
EWZ	IShares MSCI Brazil
F	Ford
FAS	Direxionshares Financial Bull 3X
FAZ	Direxionshares Financial Bear 3X
FCX	Freeport McMoRan
FDX	Fedex
FIS	Fidelity National
FITB	Fifth Third Bancorp
FLEX	Flextronics
FMCC	Federal Home Loan Mortgage
FNMA	Federal National Mortgage Association
FSLR	First Solar

FWLT	Foster Wheeler
FXE	Currency Shares Euro Trust
FXI	IShares FTSE China Index
FXP	ProShares UltraShort FTSE China 25
GDX	Gold Miners Index
GE	General Electric
GENZ	Genzyme
GFI	Gold Fields Limited
GG	Goldcorp
GGP	General Growth Properties
GILD	Gilead Sciences
GIS	General Mills
GLD	Spyder Gold Trust
GLW	Corning
GMCR	Green Mountain Coffee Roasters
GME	Gamestop
GNW	Genworth Financial
GPS	Gap
GRMN	Garmin
GS	Goldman Sachs
HAL	Halliburton
HBAN	Huntington Bancshares
HBC	HSBC Bank
HD	Home Depot
HES	Hess
HGSI	Human Genome Sciences
HIG	Hartford
HK	Petrohawk Energy
HL	Hecla Mining
HOG	Harley Davidson
HON	Honeywell
HOT	Starwood Hotels
HPQ	Hewlett Packard
HSY	Hershey
IBM	International Business Machines
IBN	Icicl Bank

INTC	Intel
IOC	Interoil
IP	International Paper
ITMN	Intermune
IWM	IShares Russell 2000 Index
IYR	IShares Dow Jones Real Estate Index
JCP	J.C. Penney
JDSU	JDS Uniphase
JNJ	Johnson and Johnson
JNPR	Juniper Networks
JOYG	Joy Global
JPM	J.P. Morgan
JWN	Nordstrom
KBH	K.B. Home
KEY	Keycorp
KFT	Kraft
KGC	Kinross
KMP	Kinder Morgan
KO	Coke
KRE	Spyder Regional Banking ETF
LCC	U.S. Airways
LDK	LDK Solar
LEAP	Leap Wireless
LEN	Lennar
LLY	Eli Lilly
LNC	Lincoln National
LO	Lorillard
LOW	Lowes
LVS	Las Vegas Sands
M	Macy's
MA	Mastercard
MBI	MBIA
MCD	McDonalds
MCO	Moody's
MDT	Medtronic
MDVN	Medivation

MEE	Massey Energy
MET	Metlife
MGM	MGM Resorts
MJN	Mead Johnson
MMM	3M Company
MMR	McMoran Exploration
MNKD	Mannkind
MNX	CBOE Mini-MNX Index
MO	Altria Group
MON	Monsanto
MOS	Mosaic
MRK	Merck
MRO	Marathon Oil
MRVL	Marvell
MS	Morgan Stanley
MSFT	Microsoft
MSI	Motorola
MT	Arcelor Mittal
MTG	MGIC Investment
MU	Micron Technology
MYL	Mylan
NBR	Nabors
NE	Noble
NEM	Newmont
NFLX	Netflix
NKE	Nike
NLY	Annaly
NOK	Nokia
NOV	Varco
NTAP	Network Appliance
NUE	Nucor
NVDA	Nvidia
NYX	NYSE Euronext
OIH	Oil Services Holders
ORCL	Oracle
OXY	Occidental Petroleum

PARD	Poniard
PBR	Petrobras
PCL	Plum Creek Timber
PCX	Patriot Coal
PEP	Pepsi
PFE	Pfizer
PG	Procter and Gamble
PHM	Pulte
PM	Philip Morris
PNC	PNC Financial
POT	Potash
PRU	Prudential
PXP	Plains Exploration
QCOM	Qualcomm
QID	ProShares Ultrashort QQQ
QLD	ProShares Ultra QQQ
QQQ	PowerShares QQQ
RCL	Royal Carribean
RF	Regions Financial
RIG	Transocean
RIMM	Research In Motion
RMBS	Rambus
RSH	Radio Shack
RTN	Raytheon
S	Sprint
SBUX	Starbucks
SD	Sandridge Energy
SDS	ProShares Ultrshort S&P 500
SEED	Origin Agritech
SHLD	Sears
SIRI	Sirius Radio
SKF	ProShares UltraShort Financials
SLB	Schlumberger
SLM	SLM Corp
SLV	IShares Silver
SLW	Silver Wheaton

SMH	Semiconductors Holders
SNDK	Sandisk
SO	Southern
SPG	Simon Properties
SPWRA	Sunpower
SPY	S&P 500 Spyder
SQNM	Sequenom
SRS	ProShares UltraShort Real Estate
SSO	ProShares Ultra S&P 500
STEC	STEC
STI	Suntrust Banks
STP	Suntech Power
STT	State Street
STX	Seagate
SU	Suncor
SUN	Sunococ
SVNT	Savient
SWN	Southwestern Energy
SYMC	Symantec
T	AT&T
TBT	ProShares Ultrashort 20 Year Treasury
TCK	Teck Resources
TEVA	Teva Pharmaceuticals
TGT	Target
TIF	Tiffany
TIVO	Tivo
TLB	Talbots
TLT	Barclays 20 Year Treasury Bond Fund
TM	Toyota
TSL	Trina Solar
TSO	Tesoro
TWX	Time Warner
TXN	Texas Instruments
TXT	Textron
TYC	Tyco
TZA	Direxionshares Small Cap Bear 3X Shares

UAL	United Airlines
UNG	United States Natural Gas Fund
UNH	United Health
UNP	Union Pacific
UPS	United Parcel Service
URE	Pro Shares Ultra Real Estate
USB	U.S.Bancorp
USO	United States Oil Fund
UTX	United Technologies
UUP	Power Shares U.S. Dollar Fund
UYG	Pro Shares Ultra Financials
V	Visa
VALE	Vale
VLO	Valero
VRSN	Verisign
VVUS	Vivus
VXX	IPath S&P 500 VIX
VZ	Verizon
WAG	Walgreens
WDC	Western Digital
WFC	Wells Fargo
WFMI	Whole Foods
WFR	MEMC Electronics
WFT	Weatherford
WHR	Whirlpool
WIN	Windstream
WLP	Wellpoint
WLT	Walter Energy
WMB	Williams Companies
WMT	Wal-Mart
WYNN	Wynn Resorts
X	U.S. Steel
XHB	Spyder S&P Homebuilders ETF
XL	XL Group
XLB	Materials Sector Spyder
XLE	Energy Sector Spyder

XLF	Financial Sector Spyder
XLI	Industrial Sector Spyder
XLK	Technology Sector Spyder
XLNX	Xilinx
XLP	Consumer Sector Spyder
XLU	Utilities Sector Spyder
XLV	Health Care Sector Spyder
XLY	Consumer Discrectionary Sector Spyder
XME	Metals and Mining Sector Spyder
XOM	Exxon Mobil
XOP	Oil & Gas Exploration & Production
XRT	Retail Sector Spyder
XRX	Xerox
XSP	S&P 500 Mini
YHOO	Yahoo
YRCW	YRC Worldwide
YUM	YUM Brands
ZION	Zion's Bancorp

Made in the USA
Charleston, SC
18 September 2013